Classroom Motivation From A to Z:

How to Engage Your Students in Learning

Barbara R. Blackburn

EYE ON EDUCATION
6 DEPOT WAY WEST, SUITE 106
LARCHMONT, NY 10538
(914) 833–0551
(914) 833–0761 fax
www.eyeoneducation.com

Library of Congress Cataloging-in-Publication Data

Blackburn, Barbara R., 1961-
Classroom motivation from A to Z : how to engage your students in learning / Barbara R. Blackburn.
     p. cm.
Includes bibliographical references and index.
ISBN-13: 978-1-59667-014-3 (alk. paper)
ISBN-10: 1-59667-014-2 (alk. paper)
1. Motivation in education—United States. 2. Effective teaching—United States. 3. Academic achievement—United States. I. Title.
LB1065.B545 2005
370.15′4—dc22

2005025194

10 9 8 7 6 5 4 3 2

Editorial and production services provided by
Richard H. Adin Freelance Editorial Services
52 Oakwood Blvd., Poughkeepsie, NY 12603-4112
(845-471-3566)

Also Available from EYE ON EDUCATION

What Great Teachers Do Differently:
14 Things That Matter Most
Todd Whitaker

BRAVO Teacher!
Building Relationships with Actions That Value Others
Sandra Harris

Great Quotes for Great Educators
Todd Whitaker and Dale Lumpa

What Great Principals Do Differently:
15 Things That Matter Most
Todd Whitaker

101 "Answers" for New Teachers and Their Mentors:
Effective Teaching Tips for Daily Classroom Use
Annette L. Breaux

Talk It Out!
The Educator's Guide to Successful Difficult Conversations
Barbara E. Sanderson

Differentiated Instruction:
A Guide for Elementary School Teachers
Amy Benjamin

Handbook on Differentiated Instruction
for Middle and High Schools
Sheryn Spencer Northey

What Successful Principals Do!
169 Tips for Principals
Franzy Fleck

Motivating & Inspiring Teachers:
The Educational Leader's Guide for Building Staff Morale
Todd Whitaker, Beth Whitaker, and Dale Lumpa

Dedication

For my dad, my first and best teacher. You believed, inspired, nurtured, and encouraged me. This book is as much yours as it is mine.

Acknowledgements

Writing a book is never an easy process, nor is it an isolated one. I would not have finished without the support of many others.

Thank you Mom, Becky, and Brenda for your understanding and patience through this process. Grandmother, I miss you. To Matthew and Jenna, it is my hope that as you grow up, you learn from many wonderful teachers.

To my friends, Janet, Karen, Gary and Susan, Chad, John, Tracy, Shane and Jan, Suzanne, Malcolm (thanks for the architect analogy), Sara, Mark, Phyllis, Don, Tom, and Betty Lou your encouragement fueled the fire.

To my colleagues at Winthrop University, it is a pleasure to work in such a supportive environment.

To David Virtue, whose tireless editing made my writing better and Melissa Miles, who is the best research assistant in the world. Her students benefit from her enthusiasm every day.

To Sam Myers for the conversations that started it all and to John Harrison for the collaboration that made it happen.

To Frank Buck, Eve Ford, Rebecca Harrison, John Keating, Tracy Smith, and Cathie West. Your suggestions helped clarify and refine each chapter. To Dave Strauss, I love the unique cover design.

To Bob Sickles of Eye On Education your patience and support throughout the process made a difference. I hope all authors work with someone like you.

To the teachers described throughout the book...your stories are inspiring.

Finally, to the teachers in my life my graduate students, those in Sumter 17 School District and at Sullivan Middle School, and all the others too numerous to list—you make a difference every day in the lives of your students.

Meet the Author

Barbara Blackburn has taught early childhood, elementary, middle, and high school age students and has served as an educational consultant for three publishing companies. She received her Ph.D. from the University of North Carolina at Greensboro. Now on the faculty of Winthrop University, she coordinates a graduate program for teachers, teaches graduate classes, supervises student teachers, and collaborates with area schools for special projects.

She has extensive experience working with K-12 teachers providing staff development in the areas of school reform, instructional strategies, literacy across the curriculum, and working with at-risk students. Topics of her published articles include literacy strategies, high-performing schools, effective communication strategies, and grading/assessment. Barbara's workshops are lively, engaging, and filled with practical, relevant information.

If you are interested in contacting Barbara Blackburn, you can reach her at bcgroup@gmail.com or at her web site www.barbarablackburnonline.com.

Table of Contents

Introduction

The inspiration for this book came from the old saying used in medical schools: "If you hear hoof beats, think horses, not zebras." It was used in response to medical students who looked for exotic diagnoses for basic illnesses.

Some teachers fall into the same trap. We look for the latest quick fix to help us deal with the ever-increasing challenges we face with today's students. The pressure to find an immediate solution that *proves* our students are learning, which is usually measured by a test score, outweighs a focus on long-term growth. Throughout this book our focus will be on the foundational, basic strategies that can assist you in developing a motivating classroom for your students. We'll be discussing the basic strategies, or hoof beats, you can integrate into everyday instruction into every subject area and across grade levels, rather than on buying a program that will fix the problem.

I'd like to address my biases up front. I am a huge believer in teachers. The daughter of a teacher and a school secretary, I taught in elementary and junior high schools; I taught beginning swimming to preschoolers and lifeguard training to high school and college students. Now I teach teachers in a graduate program at a university. Between my teaching experiences, I worked for three educational publishing companies.

I learned a critical lesson during that time: The best program in the wrong hands won't make a difference, and the worst program in the hands of a great teacher can be astounding. The solution to many of the challenges you face is not purchasing the latest program; it is a focused effort to provide your students an environment in which they can thrive.

This book does not provide you with a lockstep program, nor is it a checklist. It is a set of recommended actions that, when persistently and consistently applied, will positively impact your classroom climate. Motivation, as in the medical saying, is not exotic; it is basic, in fact as basic as ABC. As you read, you'll find 26 chapters, one for each letter of the alphabet. The chapters are not sequential, they are designed so you can start with any area that interests you or that meets a current need.

Throughout the chapters you will read stories of how teachers help their students succeed. In addition to learning about my experiences, you'll meet teachers of all ages, from preschool to college and from a variety of subject areas such as language arts, science, math, social studies, and band. The stories serve as lampposts; guiding you to new directions for your classroom.

You'll also hear the voices of students, whose names have been changed in most instances to protect their privacy. I love talking with students; they are in many ways our best teachers. If they believe you respect them and are truly listening to them, they will tell you anything you want to know.

I hope you connect with your students in new and exciting ways as you apply the strategies in each chapter and that you will also feel renewed and refreshed. As I meet teachers across the nation, I am saddened at the weariness I see. If you are tired, or if you have picked up this book because you don't feel valued as a teacher, turn to Chapter Y, You are the Key. Read it first and be reminded of your significance. Then, take a deep breath and dive into the rest of the book.

FYI

Electronic versions of selected figures and tables from this book are available at: http://www.barbarablackburnonline.com.

A

Achievement Is More
Than a Test Score

*Not everything that counts can be counted and not everything that can
be counted counts.*

Albert Einstein

Think About It...

How much pressure do you feel to ensure that your students score well
on standardized tests?

In today's age of accountability, where success is defined as a score on a
standardized test, the notion of achievement as any more than a test score can
be perceived as blasphemous. Accountability is not completely a bad thing.
I've seen positives come out of increased accountability, such as ensuring that
all students know the standards. But the notion that a score on one test given
at one time should be the only measure of whether or not someone is successful just isn't right.

I never planned to teach in a junior high school; teaching elementary school, first grade in particular, was always my dream. When a teacher transferred right after the start of school, however, my certification landed me a position teaching seventh-grade language arts and social studies. The next year I was asked to teach developmental classes, which were courses for students whose test scores were below grade level.

I was teaching eighth grade in the early years of the accountability movement. We were using a national standardized test with our students when our state decided to use those scores to determine whether or not students should be promoted to the next grade. Within the same year, the test was renormed to ensure test validity, which typically means that scores take a small dip. My students found this process extremely unfair. They were already below the cutoff score for promotion, because that was the criteria for placement in my class; the renorming process would mean that, even if they did well, their scores might go down. To them, choosing that year to start testing for promotion wasn't fair.

We had a frank discussion about the test, and we agreed on several things. First, I would do my part to help them pass the test. I would provide a daily review of test-like items and I would make sure I covered all the curriculum areas on the test before they had to take the test. Next, they would do their part, which included coming to class and completing their work. We all agreed to keep a positive attitude and do our best.

We did a daily warm-up activity that included several questions in the test format, so my students wouldn't be surprised by the types of questions they would see at the end of the year. Otherwise, I designed interesting and fun lessons around the curriculum standards. And I didn't talk much about the test other than to remind them that I knew they were going to do great! When the scores came back, most of my students scored above the cutoff and were able to move on to the ninth grade.

Today's accountability is much more rigid than what I dealt with. But the best teachers I know accept the existence of the testing and accountability movement, yet they are not limited by that reality. As Sarah Ehrman, who just finished her first year of teaching, says,

> There's a ton of pressure at our school with test scores; but if you really want better test scores, teachers need to keep doing good teaching. [We need to] establish relationships, establish a classroom environment with routines. All these other things around the actual lesson are just as important as the lesson. The students won't take it in without other things in place. Test scores may be the ultimate goal, but with students, I'm teaching things they need to learn and the standards happen to be in what I'm teach-

ing. Standards and tests are important, but if I want to be successful and be a good teacher I need to have an environment and build a relationship that allows them to learn well.

It's important to remember that student growth is never completely measured on a test. Suzanne Okey, a former special education teacher, agrees:

Achievement is supposed to be a benchmark of where students are so we understand where they are learning and where they are in development. We measure infants in every checkup: Are their heads growing enough? Can we assume they are getting adequate nutrition? It's like that in schools; we measure whether or not they get adequate nourishment. Are they benefiting from what we are providing or are we doing *one size fits all* model and leaving lots behind? We are in the business of nourishing children; nourishing their minds, bodies, and social development. Achievement looks at the tunnel of academics only. This means we are not doing the observation necessary to see if a child develops in all aspects. Then one day, you have a bright child who is doing well academically who falls off the planet because no one noticed social problems.

Our job is to help our students be successful in school, but more importantly, it's about helping them be successful in life. Great teachers define success as more than the test, and they provide multiple opportunities for every student to succeed frequently. They know that success breeds success and that all students can learn. Great teachers also teach their students that attempting something new is valuable, because even if you fail, as long as you learn and grow from the experience, you are not a failure.

What Can I Do?

The first and most foundational action you can take to create a motivating classroom environment is to minimize your focus on testing. I'm not recommending that you ignore the test; the stakes are simply too high. But you can shift the spotlight away from test scores and back to a broader view of learning. I prefer to use the word *learning*, rather than *achievement*. They may mean the same thing to some people, but I find that most teachers and students associate achievement with *the test*. So, changing my language emphasizes that I'm talking about more than test scores.

The next step is to refuse to be limited by testing. Teach your curriculum standards, but remember that you always have flexibility in how you teach them. So much frustration stems from teachers' perceptions that they lack control. You always have a choice in your lessons; you can present them in a way that is motivating and engaging and opens students' minds to the world of learning, or you can teach to the test in a boring, mundane way. It's your decision.

Finally, take a broader view of success. Celebrate every student success, not just the scores on benchmark testing. Look at the opening quote from Albert Einstein. What "counts" in your classroom? Define your view of success, and share it with your students and their families. Post it in your room, send it home in a parent newsletter, and make it a visible reminder of what you and your classroom are about. In a discussion related to test scores, a parent asked me how I would define achievement. I explained that achievement is simply your view of success. And for me, success is broader than a test score—it's about every student:

Achievement is...

S	Showcasing the
U	Unique
C	Competency and
C	Capabilities of
E	Every
S	Single
S	Student

Think About It...

How do you view success?

Summary

- Success is more than a test score.
- Be a great teacher: Provide multiple, frequent opportunities for students to succeed.
- Teach students to learn from failures and grow from the experience of failing.
- Minimize the focus on testing to maximize student motivation. Instead, focus on a student's growth and learning.
- Do not let high-stakes testing limit you—be creative and engaging while teaching your standards! Emphasize the joy of learning.

If you would like more information...

This site is about students' opinions of testing: http://www.nomore tests.com/.

Beyond Measure: Neglected Elements of Accountability in Schools edited by Patricia E. Holland, Eye On Education.

From Rigorous Standards to Student Achievement: A Practical Process by Michael D. Rettig, Laura L. McCullough, Karen E. Santos, and Charles R. Watson, Eye On Education.

B

Begin With
the End in Mind

Individuals shape their own future by creating a mental vision and purpose for any project, large or small. They don't just live day to day with no clear purpose in mind.

Stephen R. Covey

Think About It...

Before you read this chapter, write a letter or e-mail to another teacher. Imagine it's the last day of school and describe your year: all that your students accomplished, how they have changed, and what they learned from you.

As I listened to an architect friend of mine describe his job, I realized there are many similarities between his work and that of a teacher. As a teacher, you are the architect of your classroom; you design the blueprints. You might be thinking, "I don't get to design anything. I'm told what to teach, when to teach it, and sometimes even how to teach it." Architects have to deal with the same issues. They are required to follow building codes, deal with the particular attributes of the materials they use (e.g., an architect uses steel and

6

wood differently), and analyze the necessary functions of the space to generate a design that best meets the needs and vision of the client.

You must follow the education codes (accountability and/or standardized testing), accommodate the limitations of your students, and analyze the standards to generate a design that best meets the needs of your students and your vision. Four architects can use the same materials and building code but create dramatically different designs. Just as an architect begins a project with a vision, each teacher designs a distinctive classroom based on a vision. So before we get too focused on specific strategies to use with students, let's consider your classroom vision.

Vision

Stephen Covey, author of *The Seven Habits of Highly Effective People* (1989), tells a story about time management. He describes filling a big jar about halfway with sand. After putting in some small stones, he tries to add the big stones; of course, they don't fit. He demonstrates that, by putting the large stones in first, adding the small stones, and finally adding the sand, everything fits. The lesson? This is how our time works. Our calendars and days are so full of little things that are urgent, then we don't have time to do the things we value (big stones). The largest stones, the things we value the most, must be planned first, or they don't happen.

The same example works for us as we plan our classrooms. What are the stones in your classroom? The standards or the content you are expected to teach? If so, you agree with most teachers I talk with. But I think that answer is too narrow. Covey's point is that the big stones are the important things we value that get lost in the urgency of everyday challenges. In your classroom, the biggest, most important stones are the key instructional and motivational strategies that make a difference with your students, the true building blocks of learning. The smaller rocks are your standards. You know they are mandatory, and you ensure that you cover them. Finally, the sand granules are all the other activities that take up time in your classroom such as checking attendance or collecting money. It's like Covey said, you always get to the sand, but sometimes we have so much sand that we never get to the stones. There's simply not enough time left. We are so caught up in the urgency of busyness that important things don't happen.

That's how I felt when I started teaching. I was so worried about covering the material for the test and making sure I finished the textbook that I sometimes just didn't get to other important concepts. I quickly realized that many of the characteristics I wanted to develop in my students (independent learning, problem solving, creativity) needed to be the foundation for my instruction. Otherwise, they would be the *leftovers*—the important lessons I would never have time for. That's the point: If you wait to finish everything you are required to do before you use the motivational suggestions in this book, you'll never get to them. These strategies should frame how you do the things you need to do.

You may feel like the requirements to which you are held (standards and testing) are the big stones and that they are weighing you down. Again, standards and accountability serve a purpose. But *how* you accomplish them is up to you. Anyone can simply meet the requirements, similar to a checklist, but that won't promote higher levels of student understanding, nor will it encourage your students to be successful lifelong learners or problem solvers. But if you build your teaching around engaging motivational and instructional strategies, chances are you'll accomplish more; and your students will learn more. Engagement strategies, when viewed as the big rocks that go in the jar first, are not one more thing to do; they are the way to do all the things you already have to do.

Vision in Action

Do you have the letter that you wrote before reading the chapter? That is your vision for your classroom. Take another look at it, and think about how your letter for your classroom compares to the stones. In the example from Connie, a kindergarten teacher at Sunset Park Elementary School, it's easy to apply this example. One of the big stones was her use of inquiry (*always asking why*); another one is how she taught her students to internalize the school rules, rather than always reminding them of each one; and a final one is that she built a family atmosphere in her classroom where everyone works together. What are your big stones? What are the things you want to have happen by the end of the year in your classroom? That's your vision. Now, let's look at how to get there.

Dear Friend,

Here we are at the end of another year. It's hard to believe that 180 days have passed so quickly. As I look back on this year, I'm reminded what a privilege it is to teach and become a part of the students' lives for a one year. I often think that the beginning of each year is like putting a jigsaw puzzle together. Each child who walks through the door is an integral piece of the puzzle, but you wonder how each one will fit. When I reach the end of the year, everyone fits so naturally together and within the life of the classroom, it's hard to imagine all the early days trying to figure it all out.

Even taking a superficial look at the class, it is apparent that they have made gains. At the beginning of the year, success was when they would simply line up to go home in an orderly fashion. Do you remember when I told you about the first day of school and the secretary had to call down to the room to remind us to come to the bus circle? I told her, "I'm trying, but teaching kindergarten is like herding cats!" Now, they can clearly demonstrate that they have internalized the *school rules*, and they remind me when it is time to go home.

But looking deeper and thinking about their academic gains, I really get chills. They have become so accustomed to my inquiry method of instruction that they can articulate what they are thinking and why. I overheard two children talking the other day, and one said, "I know you think that, but why?" At that point that I realized that all the days saying, "Yes, that is true; but how do you know?" has paid off.

Each child has a success story to tell, but when I look at the class as a whole, the greatest success story is us! Now we are a team. We have been through so many days together that we share a common language. We have an established rhythm in the classroom, and each child knows it—even if the student marches to a slightly different beat. Just the other day, someone began the conversation, "Do you remember when?" All the children chimed in with their favorite memories of the year. Certain authors have become *friends*, and the children discuss their books as if they lived down the street.

So here we are at the end of the year….the puzzle is completed. Off they go to form another puzzle, and I'll get ready to examine new pieces.

Take care,
Connie

Instructional Planning

When I was working on my PhD, I learned about a planning model from the Dupont Corporation. The Task Cycle focuses on starting with the rationale (purpose) and desired result (product) before determining the process and resources needed. Think about how this would look in your classroom. Too often, we start with process (how to get there) and resources (what we use). We plan to have students read about spreadsheets (process) in chapter five of the textbook (resource). Then, we figure out what they should know at the end and how we'll assess their success.

Let's take the same lesson, but this time, start with the fact that it's important for students to understand how to create a spreadsheet because they can use it to plan a budget (purpose), and they'll need to apply that knowledge when they get their first job (product). Now, to do that, students need to read about setting up a spreadsheet (how), but the textbook (resource) only includes a short description that provides a definition, but no instructions. So, we also ask students to use the help section of the computer spreadsheet program and show them real-life samples of finished spreadsheets.

Try It!

Choose one of your lessons. Think about it using the Dupont Model.

Topic of Lesson/Standard:	
Purpose (Why do students need to learn this?)	
Product (What will successful learning look like?)	
Process (How will you teach this?)	
Resources (What resources do you need?)	

Backward Design

Starting with the end in mind is a hot topic in education. You've probably heard about *backward design*. The term can be used in a variety of ways, but it is simply starting with the results you want: What do you want students to know when they are finished with the year, the semester, the week, the day, or the activity? Decide how you want to measure that (what is your evidence/assessment); then determine how you want to get there. Compared to the Dupont model, it's about focusing on the product, then the process. As you think about your classroom situation, use whichever makes more sense to you.

Another simple way to think about this is a method I used when I first started teaching college courses. A professor told me if I wrote my final exam first, I would know how to plan the course. That was an eye-opener for me, and a tip that has been helpful when I plan courses. That's exactly where many of you are: Your students have a final exam, which may be one you designed or a required standardized test. If that is your product (or one of your products), what do you need to teach during the year for your students to be successful?

When I do workshops on curriculum planning, this is what I ask teachers to do. Think about what is on the final: What do students need to know by the end of the year? Next, chunk the content into more manageable pieces (typically into six- or nine- week grading periods), and map out what you plan to cover and when you want to teach it. I was in a school the other day, and kids were saying they had never seen some of the content on the test. The teacher told me she didn't have time to get to everything. She said, "You don't understand, sometimes I need to spend more time on a certain subjects because my kids don't get it, or they don't know what they should before they come to me." I understand that, but it isn't fair to test students on content that hasn't been taught. More importantly, when your students go to the next grade level, they are expected to have mastered certain standards as prerequisite knowledge for a new set of challenging information.

Chunking out your entire year helps ensure that, at a minimum, you introduce your students to the concepts they are expected to know. Think of this as an upside-down triangle, such as the one below. Use this to plan your year, then your semesters, then your grading periods, then your week, then your daily lessons. This provides a guide for you, keeps you focused, and allows you time to work on the ways to enhance your classroom experience.

Upside-Down Triangle

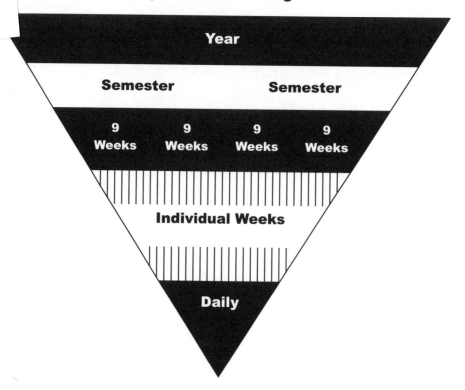

Many times, I've recommended this method to reluctant teachers, and they usually come back and tell me how they love planning this way. They have realized the benefits. First, planning from an *end-in-mind* perspective helps you see the big picture and how everything fits together. Chunking the information allows you to rearrange the content to best meet the needs of your students and sequence it to enhance learning. Some of your textbooks do this effectively, but others don't. Remember that your textbook should support your instruction, but it shouldn't drive it.

Next, having your entire year laid out in advance actually gives you more flexibility. If you need more time for review, you know how much time you can take. Simply going from day to day or week to week is like driving a car without knowing how many miles per gallon you get. When I bought a new car a few years ago, I didn't know exactly how many miles I could drive on one tank of gas. In my old car, once the low-fuel warning light came on, I could drive 80 miles before I ran out of gas. I was on my way home from a ball game in my one-week-old car, and the warning light came on. I kept thinking, "I can go 80 miles," as I tried to reach a gas station that I knew was cheaper than most of the others. Unfortunately, my new car only allows 40 miles after the warning light comes on. I know this because (you guessed it!) I ran out of gas. This is why planning your entire year is important. If you don't, you may run out of fuel before you get to the end of your trip. In other words, you may run out of time before you cover all the curriculum standards.

Finally, advance planning allows you to relax and enjoy the journey with your students. In my early years as a teacher, all my time was spent keeping up with planning. However, after I had taught for several years, and was teaching the same grade level and subject for the third time, I had a handle on the basics and could expand and enhance what I was doing. Advance planning actually allows you more flexibility, because you already know the destination. Now you can enjoy the ride, experience the scenery, and make the journey more meaningful for your students.

Summary

- Develop a vision and prioritize what matters most to you as a teacher.
- The key instructional strategies and motivational techniques you use in your classroom are the foundations for learning.
- Begin with the purpose and final product in mind, then decide the process and resources needed.
- Plan backward: yearly goals, then semester, then quarter, then unit, and then individual lessons.
- Chunk the content into manageable pieces such as six- or nine-week grading periods when planning long-term goals.
- Be flexible! Planning ahead actually helps you do this.

If you would like more information...

This site contains information on curriculum redesign:
  http://www.thirteen.org/edonline/concept2class/assessment/index.html/.

Getting Results With Curriculum Mapping edited by Heidi Hayes Jacob, ASCD.

Succeeding With Standards Linking Curriculum Assessment, and Action Planning by Judy F. Carr and Douglas E. Harris, ASCD.

Understanding by Design, Expanded 2nd Edition by Grant Wiggins and Jay McTighe, ASCD.

C

Catch Them
Doing Something Good

*Everything the teacher does, as well as the manner in which he [or she]
does it, incites the child to respond in some way or another and each response tends to set the child's attitude in some way or another.*

John Dewey

Think About It...

What is the ratio of positive to negative comments in your classroom?

Whenever I teach adolescent development, I invite Suzanne Okey, a former special education teacher, to speak to my students about working with
special needs students. Before she comes, they have one assignment: Pick a
class (or one block of time) and count the number of positive and negative
comments they make. They can make marks on a piece of paper, or they can
use two colors of marbles and move them from one pocket to another. The
process doesn't matter as long as the teachers unobtrusively keep a count.
When she starts her presentation, she asks them how they felt about the assignment. Most of the teachers say they were surprised; they didn't realize
how many negative comments they say.

Students recognize this far quicker than we do. Read one student's perspective (http://www.whatkidscando.org): "What's also discouraging is when people never mention the good things. Instead of saying 'Our geometry grades are up, we're sending kids to good colleges and stuff,' you hear, 'We only have 90% attendance, which means that 200 of you are absent.....' You know, encouragement creates encouragement. What helps is having a powerful and honest leader that we support and who supports us."

Derwin Gray, former NFL player and founder of One Heart at a Time Ministries (http://www.oneheartatatime. org), explains the impact of negative words. He points out that when we say something negative to another person, it's like hammering a nail into them. And even when we say we are sorry, which pulls the nail out, it still leaves a hole. Unfortunately, most students leave school each day with many holes in their hearts. Is that true for the students you teach?

Making a Change

How do we counter the negativity? It starts by making a choice to change your classroom's climate. My classroom was a *putdown-free zone*. No matter what was going on, no one was allowed to use sarcasm or negative comments to put down someone else. The change was amazing. It took a few weeks for everyone to get rid of the habit of using negativity as a communication tool. However, once we removed the negative, the tone of the classroom completely changed. I also became more sensitive to hearing negative comments when I was outside my room. Our society is filled with examples of negativity, some of which supposedly passes for humor. If you don't agree, pick any popular television show and count the comments. In fact, it's become so much a part of our lives, we don't even realize when we say something negative. Make your classroom a putdown-free zone and you'll be amazed at the difference.

It's not enough just to remove the negative; that leaves a vacuum. If you don't fill it with something, the negative will come back. You need to be intentional about modeling a positive attitude, sharing positive comments, and providing positive feedback. Then work to get your students on board with it, too. This is actually the easy part; once you refuse to allow negative comments, they'll join in.

Modeling a Positive Attitude

As with almost everything to do with your classroom, you must start with yourself. You attract what you project. If you want your students to have a positive attitude and make positive comments, you must do it first and you must do it consistently. Think of yourself as the mirror of your classroom. When you are hot, so are your students. If you are enthusiastic, so are they; if you are having a bad day, they will, too. If you want a positive classroom climate, it begins with your positive attitude.

Stating Positive Comments

The most visible shift you can make in your classroom is to increase the amount of praise you use with students. However, this doesn't mean to make random affirmative comments. I was in one classroom where the teacher said, "Good job!" every three seconds. Her students rolled their eyes and made faces each time. Saying good things just to say them is like doing 50 practice problems just so you can say you did them. The kids see right through you. There's a huge difference between mere catch phrases and true praise.

PRAISE

P	Personally meaningful
R	Respectful of the individual
A	Authentic
I	Immediate
S	Specific
E	Encouraging

First, praise should be personally meaningful to the student; it should be tied to something the student cares about. Next, it's important to be respectful of the individual. Some students do not like to be singled out in front of their peers. If you know that, find another way to praise them: a note, an individual comment, or even a look. As Suzanne Okey explains, "some students will appear not to respond positively to praise, then it's necessary to figure out way to deliver praise in a meaningful way to the student; give them a way to save face. In Chinese culture, saving face and losing face are huge concepts; it's big in our culture, too."

Third, praise must be authentic, or you devalue the student. If you praise Shanta when she doesn't deserve it, she'll know it, and so will everyone else.

If you think you can't find anything positive to say about David, you're not looking hard enough. Suzanne continues, "Take a correct thought, and validate that, then restate it, so he/she hears it correctly. That's what we do with students all the time; find the kernel that we can validate, then extend it; students find that very encouraging; and it creates risk-takers."

Praise also should be immediate or reasonably soon after the action being praised. If you wait two days to tell Jeremy that you are proud of him for raising his hand instead of yelling out in class, it loses its effect. Fifth, praise should be specific. Suzanne also points out, "'Good job' isn't specific. Some of our students don't know what they did that was good. They have to know what they did right; sometimes they have to know how what they did was different from what they have done before." Finally, praise should encourage the student to build on success. You want to help the student continue to move forward, and praise can be one tool to help accomplish that goal.

Providing Positive Feedback

It's also important to integrate a focus on the positive in the feedback you provide, whether it occurs informally, on a report card, or in a parent conference. I always started parent conferences by sharing the good things their son or daughter had done in class before I described areas that needed improvement. Think of it as starting off on the right foot; begin with the positive. Susan Lear, a teacher at Hartsville Middle School, involves her students in celebrating classmates' successes: "Each of my students created a short victory dance. Whenever they met a test goal or had some other accomplishment to celebrate, they were able to boogie out their excitement. This was a fun way to tap into some great talents and to keep up with the latest dance moves!"

Using Symbols

Praise should not be limited to verbal comments. Sometimes the nonverbal reinforcers, such as a smile or a look, are much more effective. Additionally, students react positively to a symbol.

Karl Kosko, a math teacher at Sullivan Middle School, found that his students responded to a new "member" of his classroom:

> I introduced Pythagorus the Goose [a stuffed animal who] loves math. He likes to watch people who are really working hard on math. So, if a group of students is working hard he might land and watch them a while. However, if they stop working hard then

he might get bored and fly off somewhere else. The reaction today was something one could see. A number of students decided they wanted the goose to come over at their table. Also, the table that ended up with the goose had some of the members encouraging others to keep working so the goose wouldn't "get bored."

Frank Buck, principal at Graham School in Alabama, tells of a school-wide effort to recognize students:

The need for a student recognition program is clear. On the other hand, the paperwork associated with them can be enough to make one think twice. The system we have used is called the "Recognition Log," which consists of a 3-ring binder with lined paper.

Recognition Log

Name	Teacher Who Recognized Me	What I Did

The notebook is housed on a stand in the main office so that it is easily accessible to students who need to sign it or visitors who would like to view it. The process is very simple. When a staff member or volunteer witnesses a student doing something worthy of positive recognition, he or she directs the student to go to the office and sign the Recognition Log. That's it! There are no special forms to distribute to staff members. Any adult, [whether] a teacher, a lunchroom worker, a custodian, an aide, or a parent volunteer, has the authority to send a student to sign the log.

About once a week, I select a name at random from the Recognition Log for inclusion on our morning intercom announcements. I read the student's name, why the student is being recognized, and the name of the adult who sent [the student] to sign the log. The student gets to come to the office to select a prize [which is usually one of those] free promotional items we all receive in the mail or pick up at conventions. I really believe our Recognition Log has impacted the culture of our school. Children routinely bring to the office money they have found, because being able to sign the Recognition Log is more meaningful than the dollar they find on the ground. They are also quick to pick up paper dropped carelessly by someone else or stop to help a student who has dropped her books all over the hallway. For a system that takes virtually no time to administer and pays such large rewards in terms of student behavior, we could not be happier with the Recognition Log.

Displaying Student Work

A final way to provide positive recognition is to display student work. However, it's important to do this in a way that students don't view it as a competition in which only the best students get their work posted. Everyone needs a fair chance to have their work on display. At Frank Buck's school, each student has his or her own "spot" in the hallway outside the classroom (in the lower grades). "That spot is labeled with the student's name and often includes a photograph of the student. Throughout the year, that student's work will appear in that same spot. Parents can walk through the hallways and know exactly where to find the work their children have produced. Our hallways are lined with cork strips, which makes the process of posting and changing out work easy."

However, students should also have a choice. If they truly don't want to post their work, they shouldn't be forced to display a product. Suzanne explains,

> I have them select their work or have input; if they choose not to have anything displayed, that's OK, but I want to figure out another way to highlight some success for that child. Some are uncomfortable about handwriting or artwork, and I don't want to force them to put out in front of world something too personal to share. Some are such perfectionists; they are never satisfied with their work. And what you don't want is for something that is intended to be positive to turn negative and engender bad feelings (such as, "mine looks so much worse than everyone else's"). That's when I turn to something that is a team effort; maybe display group work. That way, the members of group are all listed, but if a child is uncomfortable with written work, his [or her] ideas are included but not in the form of writing.

The bottom line is that it doesn't matter whether you use words, nonverbal cues, pictures, or symbols, as long as you provide positive reinforcement to your students. And don't get caught up in counting your comments everyday. I talked to one teacher who said she was a failure because she only had a five to one ratio of positive to negative comments, and some researchers recommend a higher rate. If you are making an effort to increase your positive comments, you are not a failure. As you continue to make progress; it gets easier with time and practice. And, as Dewey points out, what you do will prompt a response from your students. It's a snowball effect; your positive comments prompt their positive comments, and before long, that putdown-free zone will be a reality.

Summary

- Don't let negative comments outweigh positive ones; increase the number of genuine, positive comments.
- Don't let your classroom add to the negativity that inundates students from the media and other aspects of life!
- Let your positive attitude be contagious in the classroom!
- Praise students often with sincere, meaningful, and specific comments.
- Provide multiple opportunities for frequent, positive feedback to students and parents.
- Remember that praise can be nonverbal.
- Search for unusual, authentic ways to recognize students.
- Put student work on display. Give everyone the opportunity to share.

If you would like more information...

This site contains information on the Reinforcement Theory: http://www.as.wvu.edu/~sbb/comm221/chapters/rf.htm/.

Inviting Positive Classroom Discipline by William Watson Purkey and David B. Strahan, NMSA.

The Power of Positive Teaching by Yvonne Bender, Nomad Press.

Totally Positive Teaching by Joseph Ciaccio, ASCD.

Positive Discipline A Teacher's A-Z Guide, 2nd edition by Jane Nelson, L. Escobar, K., Ortolano, R. Duffy, and D. Owen-Sohocki, Three Rivers Press.

Negative Criticism: Its Swath of Destruction and What to Do About It by Sidney B. Simon, Values Press.

I Am Lovable and Capable: A Modern Allegory on the Classical Put-Down by Sidney B. Simon, Values Press.

D

Dealing With Diversity

We have become not a melting pot but a beautiful mosaic. Different people, different beliefs, different yearnings, different hopes, different dreams.

Jimmy Carter

Think About It...

In how many different ways can you categorize your students?

In education, we spend a lot of time labeling our students, don't we? We use gender, ethnicity, test scores, and family income level, just to name a few categories. But rather than using this knowledge to build up students, too often we use it to tear them down. Although we live in a world that is more diverse than ever, many times, we don't deal with it well.

I hear many people talk about tolerance and how we must learn to be tolerant toward those who are different from us. When we tolerate something, we put up with it temporarily until it is gone. We tolerate a toothache, back pain, and loud music coming from a neighbor's house. Why would we ever put what we do with children in the same category? Instead, we should celebrate the differences of our children.

Moving to Celebration

Celebrating diversity begins when we choose to change our attitudes. We choose to recognize that having children who are different (because each one is) is something to be valued.

My grandmother loved to make quilts. One of my most cherished possessions is a quilt she made before she died. It is a patchwork kaleidoscope of colors and patterns. I love it because it is one of a kind. There has never been one like it and there will never be. It reminds me of her, an inimitable, colorful set of surprises. She would buy scraps of cloth in different stores; she didn't go in and pick everything in advance. She picked up odds and ends and then sewed them together to make this beautiful quilt.

When you celebrate diversity in your classroom, you do exactly the same thing. You take whatever you find on that first day: Some of your children are glowing, bright colors ready to learn; others are faded and dulled by their past experiences. Do you view this as good or bad? If your response is, "Great, I can mix and match these together to make a beautiful quilt," you are already on the road to celebration. But if you think, "I need more of the bright colors, I can't really put bright and faded colors together," stop right there.

Attitude and shifting your belief is just the first step. Then, you need a strong foundation of strategies. If you celebrate, you do two things. First, you create a climate of respect and appreciation. Second, you create a support system that allows each student to thrive. The strategies throughout this book address these two goals, but let's take a moment to look at them in the specific context of diversity.

Creating a Climate

I found this quote on an Internet bulletin board: "Attitudes are 'caught' not 'taught.'" You are the first step in creating a climate of celebration throughout your classroom. You are the model that your students see each day. Rather than being uncertain or threatened by those who are different from you, start by actively modeling an attitude that embraces those differences. Kendra Alston, Academic Facilitator at Kennedy Middle School, always tells her students, "How can you learn when you are only with people like you?"

Sarah Ehrman, a high school science teacher in California, explains, "My school could not be more diverse; we're on an Army base. We have Filipino, Chinese, African American, and more. I love the diversity; there's so much you can learn from their cultures, it adds so much color to the conversation, to stories and topics. You can get so much out of that diversity instead of looking at it as too much to deal with." Her students get caught up in the same attitude.

To encourage a positive attitude toward one another, you and your students need to understand each person. One powerful way to do this is to have students write about themselves. Sarah Ehrman explains,

> My first assignment is [to ask students to write an] autobiography. It must be three typed pages, anything about themselves. Everyone wants a chance to tell their story; where they were born, about their family. They can tell me "I have a bad home situation"; or "I work long hours." They write about a sport, extracurricular activities, anything they want. They are motivated when they think you want to know about them. When I started my first job, it was because the other teacher quit (it was an inner-city school teaching the "troubled" kids). They had 15 subs before I came, and they knew they were "bad kids." One of the students told other teachers [they] were so surprised that I cared enough to have them write 3 pages and that I cared enough to read it. I did not know that would be a big deal, but it was.

Another option is to ask students to create a timeline of experiences. After the students write their individual autobiographies, you can add photos (just take digital pictures and print them) and put them in a notebook to create a class book. It's a great way to encourage students to get to know each other better by reading the book. It's also a terrific tool for new students, parents, administrators, and substitute teachers.

It's also important to talk about our similarities and differences. Often, we don't take the time to get to really know each other. Besides creating a class book about each student, create a class timeline, showcasing students' common occurrences, as well as highlighting certain unusual experiences such as band camp, travel experiences, the birth of sibling, learning a new skill, and so on. On my first day of class, I encourage students to take two minutes to learn something new about someone else in class. I challenge them to find out something unique about the other person.

After giving them several opportunities to do this, I move to one of my favorite activities, creating a physical Venn Diagram (see next page) using two jump ropes on the floor as in the following example. I pick a student to stand in one circle, then another one in the second circle. I ask students to guess what criteria I'm using to sort the students. I continue to ask students to stand in one or the other (or in the center overlap if the person fits in both categories) until they can guess my criteria. I start with something simple, such as colors of clothing or type of shoes. Then I use characteristics that aren't as visual (such as common interests). Next, I let them continue the game, sorting what they have learned. Because I give bonus points for coming up with criteria that is different and harder to guess, the students work hard to learn things their classmates have in common.

Venn Diagram

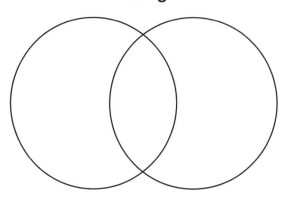

Kendra Alston chooses to teach a formal lesson on stereotypes. "For a writing activity, I give [my students] pictures, and they have to make up a name for the person, then tell about their person. They just list things; then I ask them why they put those words down. After we [discuss] it, they [write] a paper. They don't put their name on it, just a number, and they write about some of their own prejudices." She reads the final essays aloud, which prompts a richer class discussion on how we hold preconceived notions—sometimes subconsciously. This leads to a greater appreciation by her students of looking past surface labels when forming relationships with peers.

Next, focus on what kids can do, not on what they can't. I heard a special education teacher say that we should focus on abilities, not disabilities. This one is particularly important if you are working with children from a poverty background. Mark Dewalt, a colleague of mine, explains, "First, find out strengths of each child (drawing, music, listening, cooking). Second, be a good listener; both of those lead you to building relationships. Children of poverty are very good at reading nonverbal cues, so if you are doing a good job at the first two and acknowledge who they are they know the teacher cares and that impacts how they perform in the classroom."

A third way to build a climate of celebration is to ensure that every student has the opportunity to succeed, even in a small way every single day. This isn't about giving them small, silly things just so they can say they did something; this is about offering true, authentic opportunities to make daily progress and recognizing those successes for each student. Sarah Ehrman adds, "Take that theme—that all voices want to be heard; when they have a story that relates to what we are doing, make a big deal about it. Wait and listen to what students say, they will relate it to what you are teaching and then you make a big deal of it."

A Support System That Encourages Growth

Besides a climate that values diversity, celebrating diversity means providing the needed support so that each student can truly learn and grow. If we just do the basics, or teach a one-size-fits-all lesson, some students will fall through the cracks. Actually, the students who need us the most miss out. There are entire books that address the needs of specialized groups who need additional support, and I cannot do justice to those issues in one chapter. However, if you use the recommended strategies in this book to support your students' learning, you wil create a climate that celebrates diversity.

A Final Note

While writing this book, I was unsure about putting in a separate chapter on diversity. In fact, I believe we sometimes add to the discord by separating the discussion of instructional or motivational strategies for different categories of students. I agree with Franklin Thomas, who says, "One day our descendants will think it incredible that we paid so much attention to things like the amount of melanin in our skin or the shape of our eyes or our gender instead of the unique identities of each of us as complex human beings." However, there are too many people who see diversity as a way to build walls rather than bridges. So, I specifically decided to address this issue to provide a foundation for a viewpoint that permeates the entire book: Each and every child has unique learning needs. It is our job to build a relationship with our students; discover their strengths, talents, and needs; and provide the needed support to help them reach their fullest potential.

Summary

- Don't tolerate differences—celebrate them!
- Model an attitude of acceptance.
- Create a safe classroom environment where students can share openly their culture, backgrounds, and interests.
- Don't hide differences; highlight them as an opportunity to learn.
- Focus on what they *can* do—not what they can't.
- Give kids a chance to be successful every day.

If you would like more information . . .

This site contains a searchable database designed to locate resources and tools to help you meet the needs of a diverse classroom: http://equity.4teachers.org/index.php/.

A Framework for Understanding Poverty by Ruby Payne, aha! Process.

What If And Why: Ten Literacy Invitations for the Multilingual Classroom by Katie Van Sluys, Heinemann.

E

Engagement Equals Success

Love, a spirit of adventure and excitement, a sense of mission has to get back into the classroom. Without it our schools will die.

Jesse Stuart

What exactly is student engagement? I recently read a comment from a teacher on an Internet bulletin board. He said that his students seemed to be bored, and after talking with them, he realized that they were tired of just sitting and listening. He said they wanted to be more involved in their learning. I was excited to read further. The teacher said he decided then to "change how I teach, so now I make sure I do one activity each month with my class." How sad. That means 19 days each month of class with no activities. Unfortunately, that describes many classrooms today.

Don't misunderstand me. There is a place in teaching and learning for lectures and explanations and teacher-led discussions. But somehow, many teachers fall into the trap of believing that lecturing *at* or explaining *to* works. Perhaps it comes from our own experiences. Many of our teachers taught that way; it's what we saw most of the time. But how many of those teachers were outstanding or inspiring educators? Not many. I had several great teachers, and none of them taught like that. What I do remember is that the older I got, the more I was *talked at*.

Where did that idea come from—the idea that as children grow up, they should be less involved in their own learning? Let's be clear on some basic points:

- Although kids can be engaged in reading, reading the textbook or the worksheet and answering questions is not necessarily engaging.
- Although kids can be engaged in listening, most of what happens during a lecture isn't engagement.
- Although kids working together in small groups can be engaging, kids placed in groups to read silently and answer a question isn't. Activities in groups where one or two students do the work aren't engagement. Small groups don't guarantee engagement just like large groups don't automatically mean disengagement.

So, what does it mean to be engaged in learning? In brief, it really boils down to what degree students are involved in and participating in the learning process. So, if I'm actively listening to a discussion, possibly writing down things to help me remember key points, I'm engaged. But if I'm really thinking about the latest video game and I'm nodding so you think I'm paying attention, then I'm not. It is that simple. Of course, the complexity is dealing with it.

Think About It...

Take the verbal temperature of your classroom. Listen to the talking. First, subtract out all the off-task chatter that has nothing to do with learning. All of that lowers the temperature. Next, listen to the frequency of how often one person talks while everyone else is silent. That also lowers the temperature. How often are multiple people talking about learning with each other? This raises the temperature. Now, do the same thing with the level of physical activity in your classroom. How often are your students doing something productive related to learning?

I always knew I would be a teacher. In college, I focused all of my practice teaching experiences in younger grades. I just knew I would teach kindergarten or first grade. I loved reading to children; playing games with them; and most of all, I loved that look of wonder they get when they realize they have learned something new. During my methods courses in college, I spent a lot of time in early childhood classrooms working with some exceptional teachers. I have so much respect for teachers who work with young children. What

I remember most was how physically tired I was at the end of each day. Except for the morning calendar activity and story time, we never had just one activity going on. Most of the time, there were multiple centers or groups or activities.

And what I remember about the kids was that when it was nap time, they were tired—and ready for that nap. They had been so involved up to that point; they were ready for a break. In fact, one of the key *ah hah* moments for me was realizing that those teachers never gave students an opportunity to *not* be engaged in learning, and that the kids never saw it as learning. To them, it was play, and learning just happened while they were playing. That is a sharp contrast with conversations I have with many teachers. They'll say to me, "I'm doing everything I can do, but my students are bored, or they are always acting up, or they just don't seem to care." That pretty much sums up student disengagement.

I recently read Robert Fulghum's poem, *All I Ever Needed to Know I Learned in Kindergarten*, and I thought, *all I ever needed to know about student engagement I learned watching a kindergarten teacher.*

All I Ever Needed To Know About Student Engagement I Learned Watching a Kindergarten Teacher

Make it fun, and learning happens.

Build routines, and everyone knows what to expect.

Keep students involved, and they stay out of trouble.

Make it real, and students are interested.

Work together, and everyone accomplishes more.

Lesson One: Make It Fun, and Learning Happens

How much fun happens during your class? Think of it this way: If you had a choice, would you want to be doing the things you ask students to do? One of the easiest ways to make learning fun is to turn whatever you a doing into a game. I've been in classrooms that use adapted versions of Jeopardy, Bingo, Who Wants to Be a Millionaire (complete with lifelines), Wheel of Fortune, Concentration, and Trivial Pursuit. Chad Maguire uses a numeration scavenger hunt, during which students must find 50 real-world uses of math. "The students are excited to do this project, and it also opens the awareness that math is not just a subject in school." It doesn't take much to turn something into a game. Add some points and a little competition (either group or individual) and *voila*!

Erin Owens uses a popular television show to inspire her first graders:

> My students share a great deal. I have found that a microphone
> has played a key role in motivating them to produce quality
> work. First of all, they love the microphone, at first they say it is
> like "being on American Idol." You can hear them more clearly
> and their voice is obviously amplified. This gains the attention of
> the audience more so than traditional sharing. After the "glam-
> our" wears off, they begin to realize that they are showcasing
> their work each time they "step up to the microphone." I began to
> see a *major* change in their motivation to produce the best work
> they were capable of to impress and entertain their peers.

Notice how she capitalizes on her students' desire to perform to help them refine the presentation of their work.

In Texas, Karen Eliason livens up grammatical instruction with her ninth
graders by asking students to "create a play with nouns, verbs, adjectives,
etc. as characters. It was memorable, creative, and much more effective than
endless pages of drills in the textbook." As you can see, making learning fun
is not limited to any particular subject or grade level. It starts with your attitude. When you actively make learning fun, your students will have fun
learning.

Lesson Two: Build Routines, and Everyone Knows What to Expect

If someone visits a kindergarten classroom for the first time, it can seem
chaotic. There are so many actions happening at the same time, and students
are moving from one activity to another. But if you spend time there, you
quickly find that there is a structure in place. That's also true of highly effective classrooms. When students are learning, routines provide a sense of stability and predictability in the midst of activity. It is a balancing act to provide
enough variety to meet students' needs and enough structure and routine for
them to feel a sense of control and predictability. Despite any protests to the
contrary, students generally thrive when there is a clear set of rules they can
depend on and predict.

I was reminded of the importance of routines last semester when one of
my graduate students e-mailed me in a panic. The tenor of her class had
changed dramatically when the students returned from the Christmas break.
In her words, they were wild and completely out of control. As we e-mailed
back and forth, I learned that only one thing had changed: Before the holiday,
she used a warm-up activity to start each class. Students kept these in a note-

book and turned them in at the end of the week. However, she was told by an administrator that she had to take them up each day, grade them, and return them the next day. You can imagine what happened. Along with the busyness of students entering her room, she was trying to hand back yesterday's work while they were starting on today's work, and chaos followed.

I suggested she start with entrance slips. Students had five minutes to write down what they learned from the prior day's lesson and any homework. While this was happening, she handed back the graded warm-up. Next, as they started on the new warm-up, she took up entrance slips and determined how much she needed to review before she started a new lesson.

By Friday, I received an e-mail update: "My week ended so much better than it began! Entrance and exit slips are now permanent fixtures in my class. The kids have adjusted to them well. I decided to implement the slips in all of my classes, and oh what a difference they have made. I also plan to start read alouds daily…just for 5 minutes. I will begin with something that relates to some of the problems that my students may be experiencing now. I actually felt as though I was about to jump off of a cliff on Monday." Both she and her students responded well to returning to the routine with some minor adjustments.

Lesson Three: Keep Students Involved, and They Stay Out of Trouble

Beginning teachers often say they need to deal with discipline before they can focus on instruction. They quickly discover that if their instruction is busy and fast paced, many of the discipline problems disappear. Most discipline problems occur during *down time*—periods of time when students are not actively engaged in instruction, such as the start or end of class, during class changes, during lunch or recess, and during transitions between activities within your class. That's why it is so important to keep your instruction moving at a rapid pace. Don't go so fast you lose everyone, but keep it moving.

Jason Womack taught 50-minute high school classes. Each day the first task for students was to copy the schedule off the board. He organized his instruction around a theme for the day and always listed 5 to 12 activities. Typically, he scheduled 10, five-minute activities. He wanted students to see, hear, and touch something at least twice every day. In a typical day, they would "see something (watch me or data); hear about it (listen to me lecture or use the closed-eye process [tell 4–7 min. story with eyes closed]…touch something (come back from wherever they went to [in their mind] and produce something based on what they heard; draw, write it, make a video,...or a puppet show). My goal was to give them information and let them internalize and give it back; not just force-feed info and make them regurgitate it, but to give them an opportunity to internalize and express it." He also ensured that his students were constantly engaged in learning.

Tracie Clinton (Cotton Belt Elementary School) uses learning stations with her students. "When studying South Carolina (SC) the third-grade teachers arrange stations in the classrooms where students rotate. The students complete activities dealing with the various SC state symbols. We even have stations where they learn the shag, drink ice-tea, eat peaches, and make vanilla milk shakes." She also uses movement within the lesson: "When learning the South Carolina regions and counties, I create a large shape of SC on the floor. I allow the students to walk through SC to find the locations." In each of these examples, students are so busy learning, there isn't much time to misbehave.

Lesson Four: Make it Real, and Students Are Interested

Helping students make connections between their learning and real life is a foundational part of engaging classrooms. In Eric Robinson's classes at Saluda Trail Middle School, he teaches students how to write a resume. Then, he and his colleagues work together to

> show them how to select colleges/universities, the types of degrees, and job descriptions. They do a rough draft of the resume, then after we work out the mistakes, the students type their resumes along with a cover letter. Once I approve the typed resume, the students set up an interview with an administrator or teacher who is part of the interview team. Prior to setting up an interview, each student has a class in interview etiquette. In this class, the students learn how to enter the door to the interview, how to talk, eye-to-eye contact, body posture, and good communication skills with the interviewer.

Students are never too young to experience real-life learning. Erin Owens creates a fun taste of reality for her first graders. As a culminating activity for an economics unit, the class takes a field trip to a Krispy Kreme (doughnut) store. They observe real-life examples of key concepts: marketing (posters and signs), jobs (cashier, doughnut maker, and manager), goods and services, and teamwork. To apply what they learned, they set up a class store. As a group, they determined the store name, what to sell, costs and needed materials, how to market the store, and the necessary jobs. "All of this took teamwork and in the process, the students took ownership of their learning. It was amazing to see the application of concepts in progress. They had job applications [see the following example], divided into teams, and thought of everything we would need to effectively run the store. I served as facilitator and material gatherer, they planned everything. At the end, the other first-grade classes came to purchase our bookmarks."

Application

Position applying for (cashier, manager):

_____

Why do you want this job?

_____

_____

Why would you be good for this job?

_____

_____

Signed: _____

Jason Womack points out that connecting with real life is also about using students' prior knowledge to facilitate new learning.

> My favorite example of this was when I was working with a student group on World War II and postwar years testing of nuclear and atomic devices. I had a group of students [in Southern California] who were surfers, and one of the assignments that I gave for this group of students was to go and find out what the surfing was like through the 1950s and 1960s, which was when it was just starting in that community. A lot of students came back and said they did not realize how much damage was done in the Pacific Ocean around nuclear testing and atomic testing.

His purpose wasn't to make a judgment on whether the decisions about testing were good or bad; he wanted his students to think about how things impact their daily life.

Lesson Five: Do It Together, and Everyone Accomplishes More

When I was teaching, I wanted my students to work together in groups. I have always believed that we learn more together than we do alone. But my students weren't convinced. I heard more complaints about group work than anything else I did. One day, I shared a newspaper story that reported the number one reason people are fired from their job is because they can't get along with their coworkers. My students didn't believe it. They were convinced that people were fired because they couldn't do the work, so hearing that getting along with others was an important part of working was new information to them. After that, I met less resistance to group activities.

Connie Forrester, a kindergarten teacher, explains, "It is important to me that I provide opportunities for learning that are authentic and based on a framework of inquiry. I believe children will be more motivated to accomplish a task that feel makes sense and is meaningful....Group work is one way I achieve this goal. I work hard all year to help the children see we are part of a team that all that we accomplish as individuals affects all that we accomplish as a group." That's the key to effective group work: students working together around an authentic task, building on each other's strengths!

Summary

- Engagement means active involvement in the learning process.
- Never give students an opportunity to be unengaged.
- Make your activities fun and appealing, and learning will happen.
- Clear structure and routines can establish healthy, effective, learning environments.
- Don't let *downtime* be a door for discipline disasters; keep students continuously involved in instruction.
- Keep student learning real, and help them make connections to their own lives.
- Provide frequent opportunities for students to collaborate with peers. We all learn more together than we do alone.

If you would like more information...

This site is about cooperative learning: http://edtech.kennesaw.edu/ intech/cooperative learning.htm/.

This site is about constructivism and the Five Es: http://www.miamisci. org/ph/ lpintro5e.html/.

This site is about inquiry-based learning: http://www.thirteen.org/ edonline/concept2 class/inquiry/index.html/.

Active Learning: 101 Strategies to Teach Any Subject by Mel Silberman, Allyn and Bacon.

Applying Standards Based Constructivism: A Two-Step Guide for Motivating Elementary School Students or Applying Standards-Based Constructivism: A Two Step Guide for Motivating Middle and HS Students by Pat Flynn, Don Mesibov, Paul J. Vermette, and R. Michael Smith, Eye On Education.

Cooperative Learning: Theory, Research, and Practice (2nd Edition) by Robert E. Slavin, Allyn & Bacon.

The Classroom of Choice: Giving Students What They Need and Getting What You Want by Jonathan C. Erwin, ASCD.

F

Form Partnerships

If we are together nothing is impossible. If we are divided all will fail.

Winston Churchill

Most of this book describes specific strategies you can use directly with your students to engage them in learning. But in this chapter, we are going to broaden our focus to those who are connected with your students. Ginny Markle, former president of the national Parent-Teacher Association (PTA) points out that children and adolescents need at least five caring adults in their lives. I am assuming if you are reading this book you are one of those five caring adults in your students' lives, and this chapter is about forming partnerships with the others to maximize each student's potential.

Think About It...

Identify the caring adults for each of your students. Start with family members (parents, siblings, grandparents, etc.). Second, think about former teachers your students loved and responded to. Next, think of other activities your students participate in and the associated adults (coaches, club sponsors, church). Finally, are there other adults in your school who can provide support (counselor, administrator, etc.)?

There are three questions that should frame your actions as you form partnerships with the other adults in your students' lives:

1. What can *you learn from them* to support your student better? This might include information about how the child learns best or any special interests and needs.

2. How can *you help them*? Daniel enjoyed working on the school newspaper, particularly drawing editorial cartoons. His math teacher was a friend of mine, and she shared that Daniel did not always complete his homework, which caused him to fall behind. The three of us agreed that if he didn't do his math homework, she would let me know about it and he would leave my class to go catch up his homework in her class. This worked especially well because journalism was an elective course, but the main reason it worked was that he wanted to be in my class, so he finished his homework.

3. How can *they help you*? Several of my struggling readers played on our junior varsity football team. The students and I talked with their coach about what they needed to do in my class to be successful. He then monitored their progress in class, and checked in with me regularly to offer additional support. It was a turning point for those boys.

For simplicty, I'm going to use the word *parents* as I discuss how to form partnerships, but these strategies apply to any of the caring adults in the student's life.

Forming and Strengthening Partnerships

During my first year of teaching, one of the other teachers in my school stopped by my room. I was making a list of parents because I had decided to call every one during the first month of school. He just laughed and told me I was definitely a new teacher. Then, he said, "You really don't have time to deal with parents in addition to everything else you need to do. Pay attention to your lesson plans and don't worry about parents until they call you." As I continued to work with him, I realized his perspective came from the things *not* to do, rather than what to do. I learned to do the opposite of what he recommended, and I developed four guidelines for developing partnerships.

Guidelines

Partnerships are our responsibility

Shine a light on your classroom

A true partnership is a two-way street

Feedback facilitates the partnership

Partnerships Are Our Responsibility

Many partnerships are destroyed before they start, because the teacher believes it is someone else's responsibility to prompt a connection. This was exactly the attitude of my former colleague. If you believe it's the parents' responsibility to communicate and/or follow-up with you, that attitude comes through when you talk with them. Communicating with parents is not an extra job; it is part of your job. There is no way you can truly help your students be successful without the support of their parents. And it's up to you to take the first step.

I called every parent during the first month of school to introduce myself and tell them something positive about their son or daughter. I thought of parent relationships like a bank; I needed to make a deposit before I made a withdrawal. I didn't want my first phone call to be the one about a poor grade or a discipline problem. One time it took 17 calls to reach a parent before I was finally successful. It took about five minutes to convince her I wasn't calling because Marcus was in trouble. She finally said she had never received a call from a teacher telling her something positive about her son. She thanked me and immediately offered her help anytime I needed it. Five weeks later when Marcus was in trouble in class, she supported me 100%. It's our responsibility to connect with parents; and the benefits outweigh any costs in terms of time.

Suzanne Okey, a former special education teacher, agrees:

> In terms of families, I'm big on home visits. I feel like it's always fair to get off your turf and go into the environment where they are most comfortable. It says this is a two way street; I'm not expecting you to make all the accommodations; I'll meet you where you are. If teachers truly want to form partnerships, they cannot expect it all to be "come to me"; you have to be willing to go to them. Sometimes I sent a letter. It is important to give them options, such as meeting them in neutral places (the public library or McDonald's) in order to preserve their privacy and dignity. Not

everyone has transportation or telephones, and they don't want to advertise that to world.

Shine a Light on Your Classroom

When I talk to parents, many of them feel as though there is a hidden code in schools; a code they don't understand. Margo and her son moved to a new area when Jared started middle school. She missed the first parent-teacher meeting because she was working. She called the school and left several messages asking to meet with his teachers, but didn't receive a return call. Margo was frustrated when she told me her story. Another teacher at the school was in one of my classes, so I talked with her. I discovered that the school had a policy that all appointments with teachers were scheduled with the attendance secretary, so the entire teaching team could meet with parents without scheduling conflicts. My graduate student said the principal always explained the policy at the first meeting. So of course, Margo didn't know because she wasn't at the meeting, and she thought the teachers were just ignoring her. One phone call later, she connected with the teachers, and she and Jared finished the year successfully.

Building partnerships is never about secrets; in fact, part of the process is helping each partner understand what is going on in your classroom. In a later chapter I discuss developing a sense of ownership in your students; but you also want parents to feel that they are truly a part of your classroom. And that can't happen if they don't know or understand what you are doing. Kendra Alston (Kennedy Middle School) believes that communication is an important part of her job. During the first two weeks of school, she guides her students as they create a brochure for parents about their classroom.

"The students do all preliminaries, I just put it together. I tell them my philosophy, then each block gets together and comes up with quote that describes their class. It also includes a poem I write to parents every year that finishes by asking for support from them. I always finish with the message that I can't do anything without you." She also sends a brochure that informs parents of basic information they need during the year, including her contact information, grading and homework information, and any other relevant classroom policies (see the sample Brochure).

Brochure

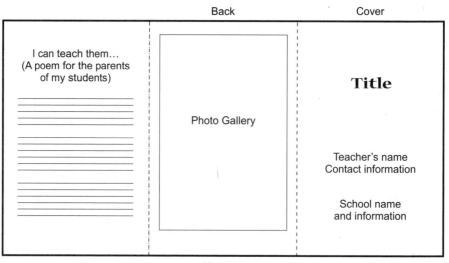

Back   Cover

I can teach them…
(A poem for the parents
of my students)

Photo Gallery

Title

Teacher's name
Contact information

School name
and information

(Outside)

(Inside)

Mission Statement/
Classroom Philosophy

How will I know what's
going on in the classroom?

What is your discipline policy?

What will my child
learn this year?

How will my child be
graded this year?

Our schedule

A True Partnership is a Two-Way Street

So far, I've focused on communication from school to home, but a partnership is more than that. Although it's our responsibility to take the initiative to form partnerships, everyone has a role. I've found that most parents are willing to help, but they need specific ways to help.

Kendra sends home an interactive newsletter every two weeks. Besides the information, there is a question for the parents to answer and send back. She has a high return rate because students receive points for returning the newsletter. She also uses interactive homework. "For example, I'll take a picture of something my students did in school. Then, I write 'ask me what I learned today' at the top of the page. The parents have to write what their son or daughter said. This lets me know if the students even remember what happened. I'm also always about getting feedback on my own performance and when the parent writes a reflection on what their child is learning, it gives you insight on how well you taught."

It's also helpful to provide parents a list of ways they can help at home. This should include clear guidelines of what constitutes appropriate help (doing their science project for them isn't) and any other simple tips (see *Tips for Parents*). Many elementary schools send home a monthly calendar to post on the refrigerator. Each day has a simple activity families can do together.

Tips for Parents

- Encourage your child to give 100% at all times.
- Reinforce concepts and habits the teacher is trying to build. If Johnny is learning how to multiply percents at school, have him help you calculate the tip at a restaurant.
- Encourage your child to set a designated time when homework will be completed every day.
- Provide a quiet, well-lit environment at home with all of the materials necessary for completing school tasks (extra paper, scissors, pens, pencils, pencil sharpener, a dictionary, markers, highlighters, a ruler, calculator, index cards, etc…).
- Prevent brain freeze—allow your child to take a short break every thirty minutes or between homework tasks.
- Be careful not to give answers to homework questions; instead, offer advice about where to look for an answer.
- Model what productive work looks like. When your child does homework, you do yours too (balance a checkbook, pay the bills, etc…).

Feedback Facilitates the Partnership

One of the most valuable parts of a partnership is the opportunity to receive authentic feedback for improvement. Kendra mentioned that her interactive homework actually helps her understand the effectiveness of her lessons. She also sends a feedback slip home with students' weekly folders. It's an easy, informal way for parents to communicate with her regularly. She also uses these with her students, and with anyone who attends her workshops (see the sample *Feedback Form*).

Feedback Form

Please stop…
Please start…
Please continue…

By now, you've realized that Kendra focuses a tremendous amount of attention on partnerships with parents. I've never met a teacher who is so intentional about asking parents for feedback. Besides the informal feedback, she has parents complete a report card on her each grading period (see the example on the next page). "I send it home and the parents score me and add comments. Sometimes I get some twos, especially from some with kids who struggle. But, the parents love that. I get all of them back, because the kids get points for returning them. They don't have to make comments, but I encourage it. The benefit comes from establishing a rapport with parents."

Yes, it takes time and attention to build partnerships with the adults in your students' lives. You may not be able to connect with everyone for each of your students. In that case, prioritize. Build at least a basic relationship with the parents of all your students, then focus on those who need some extra attention from you. And don't feel like you have to start by doing everything I've described here. I know if I was in a classroom today, I wouldn't start with having parents fill out a report card on me. I'd begin with a brochure, interactive homework, and informal opportunities to provide feedback. Then, as I built a relationship with the parents, I'd move to some of the other ideas. But, through it all, I'd keep my focus. Paraphrasing Winston Churchill, "If we are together nothing is impossible. If we are divided all [insert student's name] will fail."

Report Card for Parents

Code	
4	Exceeds expectations
3	Meets expectations
2	Sometimes meet expectations
1	Does not meet expectations
SP	Shows progress from last report

Curriculum	1	2	3	4	Comments
▪ Displays knowledge of subject matter.					
▪ Develops and implements lessons to meet my child's performance level.					

Effective Communication	1	2	3	4	Comments
▪ Responds in a timely manner.					
▪ Communicates in various ways (i.e., e-mail, telephone, face-to-face, notes, etc.).					
▪ Listens to parent's concerns and work cooperatively to solve problems.					

Classroom management	1	2	3	4	Comments
▪ Practices fairness and consistency.					
▪ Demonstrates good organizational skills.					

Efforts	1	2	3	4	Comments
▪ Encourages parent participation.					
▪ Suggests resources as needed.					

Summary

- Students need to be surrounded by adults who genuinely care for them.
- Reaching out to parents is part of your job as a teacher. It is *not* their responsibility to track you down.
- Do not keep secrets from parents. Speak honestly and sincerely in a language they can clearly understand.
- Most parents are ready and willing to help—you just need to show them how!
- Allow parents opportunities to provide you with authentic feedback.
- Start with small steps to make your parents feel welcomed and appreciated. It takes time to build partnerships with the adults in your students' lives.

If you would like more information...

This site is the home of the National Parent Teacher Association (PTA): http://www.pta.org/.

This site offers advice on making Family and Community Connections: http://www.thirteen.org/edonline/concept2class/family community/index.html/.

How to Involve Parents in a Multicultural School by Bruce Davis, ASCD.

Teacher Talk! The Art of Effective Communication by Cheli Cerra and Ruth Jacoby, Jossey Bass.

G

Goals and Success

Mutual commitment helps overcome the fear of failure—especially when people are part of a team sharing and achieving goals. It also sets the stage for open dialogue and honest conviction.

Coach Mike Kryzweski

Society focuses much attention on goal setting. You can read books, listen to tapes, attend seminars, or see programs on television about having a goal-oriented attitude, setting and achieving goals, and balancing your life through prioritizing goals. We do the same thing in education. In fact, just about everything we do is founded on goals, particularly long-term goals. When students ask why they must learn whatever you are teaching that day, the answer is usually "Because you'll need it later in life," "It's on the test," or a similar response. We expect students to spend their time pursuing goals they may not even want.

I'm not going to say to quit teaching concepts students need later. What I am going to suggest is that we frame learning and goal setting in terms students can understand, and hopefully, in a way they can use to set personal learning goals. We also have to recognize that, for some students, our goals are not their goals. We may want them to love reading or make good grades, but they may be focused on impressing you, or making Mom and Dad happy, or playing for the National Basketball Association (NBA). My typical response to that goal is, "That's great. When that's over after five years, and you've made your millions but still need money (true for many former NBA players), what do you want to do?" To some degree, we are looking for a balance of our goals for them and their own personal goals. Teaching goal setting can start with even the youngest children (lining up quietly, listening quietly to a story), and it builds as they get older. Good goals provide direction and may help students make good choices, rather than leaving them susceptible to peer pressure and following the crowd.

SMART Goals

Students need to set and achieve goals to build a sense of confidence, which leads to a willingness to try something else, which in turn begins a cycle that leads to higher levels of success. Success leads to success, and the achievements of small goals are building blocks to larger goals.

Success Cycle

I like the model of setting SMART goals because they are simple and understandable for students.

SMART

S	Specific
M	Measurable
A	Attainable
R	Realistic
T	Timely

Let's look at how this works with students' goals. Peter is a high achiever who wants to be perfect. In fact, if you ask him for his goal, he'll say it is to be a perfect student. But that isn't specific or measurable because perfection is subjective and difficult to measure. It is probably not attainable or realistic because perfection is such an elusive goal; and it isn't timely because there is no end date. This sets Peter up for failure, because there is way to achieve the goal and move on to the next one.

Think About It...

How could you help Peter turn his goal into a SMART one?

I also like the SMART goals approach because it forces you and/or your students to break down the specific steps needed to achieve the goal. I watched a parent respond to the following comment from a teacher: "Your daughter needs to study harder to do well in my class." He replied, "My daughter *is* studying hard. What do you mean study harder?" This parent was looking for actions he could control, and the vague nature of the statement frustrated him. It is more helpful to describe the specific next actions to take. Think of items on a list that can be checked off when they are completed.

We know what those are. By *study harder,* we really mean things like read the text selection, take notes in class and study them at home; do your homework every night and if you have a question, first try to find the answer, then ask the teacher; and don't wait until the last minute to work on a project, work on it a little every night. The problem is that we don't always say these things to parents or students, or we say them once and don't provide further reminders.

Student Goal-Setting Activities

A good place to start is to talk about goals with students. You can share one of your goals, and discuss their goals. You may have to start broader with dreams, and then focus on the specific goals. I visited a classroom that had a large bulletin board titled *Our Goals.* Each student wrote his or her goal and posted it for everyone to see. Many wrote the standard "make good grades," but some wrote more personal ones. Other options are to have students write about their goals in journals. The point is to have them identify their own goals and for you to know about them so you can tie learning to their goals.

> *I want to make it out without any conflicts and working toward being a model and designer. I will do my best to follow directions.*
>
> Shayla

I used two different goal-setting activities when I was teaching. First, each of my students created a "Me Poster" at the start of the year. I adapted this idea from one my dad used with teachers during workshops. I provided some starting points using basic pictures or shapes (see Components of *Me Poster*), and they could customize the posters. This gave me a tremendous amount of information about who they were and their interests and goals—probably more than I would have known if I had merely talked with them, or even asked them to write about themselves because many were reluctant writers.

My students and I also enjoyed creating time capsules for each person using paper towel cardboard rolls. At the start of the school year, I asked them to focus on where they were in terms of academics, accomplishments, or interests. Students selected objects that represented different things about themselves, and they put those objects in the tube along with an essay they wrote. They told about themselves using the contents, then filled the tube and decorated it. I hung the tubes in the classroom, and at the end of the year, my students opened them and wrote a new essay about how they had changed over the year. Many of them were surprised at how much they had learned and grown.

Components of *Me Poster*

Star	In what way do you star as a student?
Trading Stamp	What part of your personality would you like to trade in?
Flower Pot	How can you make our classroom a better place to be?
First Prize Ribbon	For what one thing would you like to be remembered?
Crown	What is your crowning achievement?
Winner Sign	Why are you a winner?
Turkey	What are the turkeys that get you down?
Question Mark	What one thing do you want others to know about you?

Breaking Down Next Steps

Once students decide on a goal, it's important to spell out the steps to reaching a goal. David Allen, author of *Getting Things Done,* insists that detailing the next action to be taken is an important part of achieving our goals. I may want to be a writer, but to actually become one doesn't just happen; there are specific actions I need to take. Too often, we take such a global approach to learning; our students don't understand the specific steps to achieving a target. We need to help students identify the exact next step to accomplishment. What exactly do they need to do next? If they want to make an A in science, and there is a test on Friday, the next steps might include reading the description of the parts of a plant, labeling a diagram of a plant, taking the diagram home to study, and studying the diagram. Some of your students do this automatically, but others need your help to be successful.

On a visit to Reid Ross Classical School, I stepped into a seventh-grade classroom. A series of t-shirts caught my eye, and the students wanted to share their completed projects with me. A short conversation quickly turned into a modeling session with students wearing the shirts and showing off their dreams. Mrs. White explained that, as part of a celebration of Martin Luther King's life, she discusses his dream for all people. Students are given project guidelines, and they have approximately a month to complete their shirts. On the front of the shirt they illustrate their dream using fabric paints, computer design graphics or any type of embroidery. On the back, students write the steps to achieving their goal, which is based on their own research. It was an excellent way for students to learn the next steps required to achieve their goals.

Goals for the Future: Jobs and Careers

When I was in high school, I remember attending a *Career Day,* when different people came into my school and talked about their jobs. It was a one-shot attempt to expose students to a variety of options for the future. Today, most schools I work with integrate a focus on jobs and careers into the overall curriculum. And it is no longer something that waits until middle or high school; there is an early focus on using learning in future jobs.

This can happen in formal or informal ways. For example, I met a second-grade teacher who told me she reads simple biographies to her students, particularly highlighting people her students might not know, such as Mae Jemison, the first African American female astronaut. Many teachers will assign students to research a particular job or career. Other teachers simply discuss careers or jobs when it links to a specific lesson.

For example, a math teacher wanted his students to build a spreadsheet. Rather than just asking them to use random numbers, he asked his students to pick a job they might want to do, find out how much the job would pay, then set up a budget based on that income. The resulting posters were meticulous; students detailed out the gross and net pay; the amount for federal, state, and local taxes; and an itemization of the budget expenses (including rent, a car payment, etc.). This was a lesson that allowed ample opportunities for students to practice math skills and to relate those skills to real-life situations.

When attending a conference several years ago, a teacher shared with me a story of a teacher in Wilmington, North Carolina, who used the aspirations of her male students to teach a great lesson. When Wilmington native Michael Jordan was extremely popular, all her boys wanted to be like Michael. Rather than discouraging them, she taught them about all the skills he used in his job. First, he used knowledge of geometry when determining the best angle for shooting the ball. He also used a variety of math skills to manage his money. When the students said they would pay someone to do that for them, she countered that they needed to know enough to make sure the person they paid was doing the job correctly. Finally, she explained that Michael Jordan required a variety of communication skills to deal with the media.

Jason Womack, a former middle and high school teacher, used a more formal approach with his students, called *Wednesdays With Womack*. Students volunteered for the 16-week extracurricular program, and they did not receive grades or extra credit. Jason went into his local community in Ojai, California, to find people willing to eat lunch with his students and share 3 things:

1. What do you do?
2. How did you get there?
3. How do you plan for success?

He purposely avoided asking lawyers or police officers to come in. As he told me, "They get enough of that on TV." He chose people such as the entrepreneur of most successful coffee shop in town or a guy who started out as an architect, moved into contracting, and was then a venture capitalist who built shopping malls. He also brought in Denzel Stiegelson, the stage manager for Paul Simon; the executive director of Ronald Reagan Presidential Library; and a local author who wrote about financial freedom for teenage girls. He was surprised that most people were willing to come and share; all he needed to do was ask. To open his students to more opportunities, he sought out people with jobs that were less traditional. For example, one guest studied the Abaloni shell population off the coast of California.

For five minutes after the guest finished, Jason and his students would debrief. It was a short discussion in which students would talk about what they learned, what they still wanted to know about the person or job, and whether or not they would want to listen to that person again. How did his students respond? Almost every week they had the same comment: "I can't believe they get paid for that." Jason was intentional about showing students a broader view of options for the future.

Short-Term Goals

We've spent a lot of time talking about long-term goals, and those are important. However, for many students, particularly those living in poverty, taking the long-term view is ineffective. When you survive from day to day, thinking about the future isn't a part of your frame of reference. And even if I am focused on a big goal for the future, I need to have a sense of accomplishment of more immediate goals to keep my momentum. Some of your students need daily goals along with positive reinforcement for achieving them; others thrive with weekly goals. This depends on the age, maturity level, and self-confidence of your students. As with most things, you will need to adapt these ideas to meet their individual needs.

One tool to assist with planning and following through with specific next actions is a student agenda. Frank Buck, principal of Graham School in Talladega, Alabama, explains, "We have used student planners for several years beginning with first grade with great success…. If we can get students in the habit of using the planner as their central place to capture homework assignments, info on stuff going on in their classroom and throughout the school, and info on their personal appointments, we have done a pretty good job. We also stress to parents that if they only do one thing to help their child, let it be look at the planner. That's going to be the spot the teacher wrote a two-sentence note to Mom instead of on a scrap of paper that winds up 17 layers down in the book bag." The agendas help students identify and collect all the next actions they need to accomplish.

Many schools use student agendas or planners, which is a lively topic on some education-oriented Internet bulletin boards. As I reviewed the comments, the most piercing complaint comes from parents who say that schools just give them out and don't teach students how to use them successfully. That's a valid point, and one we need to address. Using an agenda to set goals and track progress or for communication is like any other new skill; there is a learning curve. We should not assume students know how to use them just because we tell them how one time.

The students who use planners most effectively talk about how their teachers taught them how to use the agenda as a tool and then provided follow-up instruction and reminders of the important points. TSpall, a teacher posting on a bulletin board, wrote, "We try to encourage students to use them to keep up with their assignments. Each teacher has an assignment board where all things they need are written out. It's an example for them to follow until they (hopefully) start to record their own."

Celebrating Successes

Finally, it's critical to celebrate successful completion of goals. In our time-pressed culture, we sometimes forget to pause and commemorate our accomplishments. However, this is part of the success cycle I mentioned earlier. When students succeed in accomplishing a goal, they are more confident and more willing to set future goals. Celebrations serve as memory markers for students; guiding them to the next level of success.

Summary

- Frame learning and goal setting in terms your students can understand.
- Set goals to help students make wise choices and provide them with direction.
- Help students set goals that are specific, measurable, attainable, realistic, and timely.
- Implement activities in the classroom to help students set goals and track their progress toward them.
- Use learning contracts to help students feel ownership over their own learning.
- Show students how to break goals down into small steps.
- Use adults in the working force to come in and discuss real-world careers and the goals that got them there.
- Use agendas or planners, which are a great tool to help students keep track of their goals because students thrive on short-term goals.
- Don't forget to stop and celebrate success!

If you would like more information...

This site is a guide for setting goals and becoming motivated: http://www.goal-setting-guide.com/.

Getting Things Done by David Allen, Viking.

Goal Setting 101: How to Set and Achieve a Goal! by Gary Ryan Blair, Blair Publishing House.

Goal Setting for Students by John Bishop, Accent On Success.

Goal Setting for Success by Jerry Rottier and Kim Libby, National Middle School Association.

What Do You Really Want? How to Set a Goal and Go for It! A Guide for Teens by Beverly K. Bachel, Free Spirit Publishing.

H

High Expectations
for Everyone

You see, really and truly, apart from the things anyone can pick up (the dressing and the proper way of speaking, and so on), the difference between a lady and a flower girl is not how she behaves, but how she's treated. I shall always be a flower girl to Professor Higgins, because he always treats me as a flower girl, and always will; but I know I can be a lady to you, because you always treat me as a lady, and always will.

Eliza in George Bernard Shaw's *Pygmalion*

Think About It...

Think about your worst student (or, if you teach multiple classes, your worst class). Write the name of your student or class at the top of a sheet of paper. Now, draw a line dividing the paper into two columns. In the first column, I want you to write down everything positive about that student or group of students. Make a list (time yourself, write for at least five minutes) of every single positive thing you can think of. Finished? In the second column, take five minutes to write down every lesson, teaching or discipline strategy, or comment that has ever worked with this student or group.

Which list was harder to make? If you said the first one, this chapter is for you; because, like Eliza in *Pygmalion*—or the popular version *My Fair Lady*—reality for students has as much to do with how other people view them as it does with how they view themselves. If you had a worst student or class (and some people tell me they can't come up with one), it is reflective of an underlying negative perception, and even if it is deserved; this subtly impacts what you do and how you work with your students.

Having high expectations starts with a choice: You decide that every student you teach is a jewel with the potential to be the best—no matter what. Yes, sometimes this is hard, and I've struggled with particular students, too; but I've always remembered that students live *up to* or *down to* your level of expectation for them.

This was especially true for me with Patricia. Before I met her, three teachers came to see me to tell me how sorry they were that I would have her in class. I'm ashamed to admit to you this shaded my perspective of her. I was nice to her, but I was always waiting for her to do something. After all, she had done so many bad things in other classes. The day I realized I was treating her with a little less care than with other students, I vowed to stop. I gave her extra attention, made sure to praise her when she did something well, and encourage her when she was struggling. She became one of my best students.

That happens. Sometimes we send messages subconsciously. For example, we expect girls not to do as well with math, or we think our boys won't like to read as much as our girls. Or, because Meaghan's older brother was a great writer, we don't understand why she isn't a great writer, too. I've heard teachers say, "I try to cover harder material, but they just can't handle it; they should have already known this, but I had to go back and review." These attitudes prevent students from reaching their full potential. We get what we expect. And students recognize this much quicker than we do.

I was at a middle school in Maryland and had a delightful conversation with Gabrielle. My favorite question to ask students is, "If you were in charge of the school, what would you change?" Her answer was so insightful. She said, "for people who don't understand as much...[they should] be in higher level classes to understand more [because] if they already don't know much, you don't want to teach them to not know much over and over." Isn't that reflective of how students view our levels of expectations in classes that are not higher level?

Yes, But...

In some ways, an attitude of low expectations sneaks up on us. I call it the *yes* (*but*) mentality. When I talk to teachers and principals about change and make a recommendation based on something I've seen in schools, many times I get the enthusiastic *yes*, we should hold all students to high expectations, then the cautious, "*but* that wouldn't work here because...." What I know is this: If there's a *but* at the end of your comment about students, your expectations are lowered. Finding the buts is easy: "We can't...." "Someone won't let me...." "He or she doesn't have whatever...." "I've tried that...."

Recognize that *but* is just another word for failure. I'm recommending you monitor your own language, and every time there's a *but*, replace it with the *here's how* (see Common Excuses Table). So, "Yes, we should have high expectations, and *here's how* I'm going to try that today. Yes, we need to do more individualization with our students, and *here's how* I think we could make that work given our circumstances. Yes, our kids don't see many positive role models at home, and *here's how* we can address that as a school."

Common Excuses
That Subtly Encourage Lowered Expectations

Situation	Negative Response	Positive Response
Students aren't doing homework	But they just don't do it	Here's how I can find out what is really going on and help them turn in their work
Students just don't seem motivated	But I've tried everything I know how to do	Here's what I'm going to try again today...
Students misbehave	But they are just that way (it's because they are in middle school, etc.)	Here's how I'm going to adjust what I am doing to better meet their needs

Wow! See how just changing that one word makes a difference? I'm not saying you have to know all the answers. One of my favorite instances of this was when a teacher said to me, "I don't know what to do about my kids, *but* I'm willing to learn and try!" That's one of the few times I've heard it used in a positive way.

Don't misinterpret what I'm saying; of course your kids have to do their part. However, when I talk to someone about school improvement and they agree, *but...*, that limiting attitude shines through to the kids. When I go into classrooms where teachers are making a difference with the toughest kids, there is a no-excuses attitude; one that says, "We are here to move forward, and there are no excuses that will stop us." The word *but* is a big stop sign in the road to high expectations. As Jason Womack said, "For me to think that kids can't learn something [is unthinkable]...."

Think About It...

Are there subtle beliefs or comments that undermine your efforts to raise student expectations?

Equal Treatment for All?

Clearly, we should have high expectations for all students. However, I want to spend a few moments discussing those students who need extra attention from you related to this area. Jack, a fourth-grade teacher, expressed a typical frustration: "I have twenty-six students. So don't tell me that I need to do all kinds of extras with every one of them. I'm already doing all I can do."

You teach a few students (it may be one, two, or five) who need something extra from you. These students may not have a stable home life, they may not have family members who hold them to high expectations, or they may have a history of poor grades or a reputation as a troublemaker. I'm challenging you to invest additional efforts with those students.

When I shared this perspective in a workshop, one parent was quick to tell me that it is every teacher's job to treat every child equally. As I read news stories about education issues, I find that many people say they believe in equal treatment for everyone; of course, unless they are the ones benefiting from special attention. But it is my experience that equal is not always the best choice. One of my favorite quotes is: "Nothing is more unequal than equal treatment of unequal people" (often accredited to Thomas Jefferson but not attributed to him by Jefferson researchers). That completely sums up my attitude. I believe that some students come to us needing more than others do. You teach students without books or other resources at home, and you teach students with everything they could ask for. You have some who receive encouragement and love everyday and others who are lucky to hear a positive word from someone they know once a month. Which ones need a little more from you?

If you choose to invest in those students who need more from you in this area, I'd ask you to *Expect the BEST*, which means investing in them in four specific ways: belief, encouragement, support, and time.

Belief

The most basic characteristic to invest in your students is a strong belief that they are important, valued, and capable. As Coach Mike Kryzweski says, "Confidence shared is better than confidence only in yourself." During a visit to Reid Ross Classical School, Principal Diane Antolak explained that she personally reviews all student schedules. If she sees a student has not registered for advanced classes and she believes the student should be in a higher level class, she changes the schedule, then sets up a meeting to discuss the change. I wanted to hear the students' perceptions of this process; they were quick to tell me how much they appreciated it. They were overwhelmingly positive, and as one young man said, "It makes me work harder, because I know she believes I can do the work." Sharing your belief in a student is a powerful motivator.

Encouragement

Anatole France says that nine-tenths of education is encouragement. Think of encouragement as the wrapping paper for your present of belief. Students who do not have a lot of self-confidence need a steady stream of encouragement. When you plant a new tree, you need to regularly water it so it will grow. That's what encouragement is for your students. Encouragement can be as simple as a smile or a few extra words written on a test, but it is always a signal to the student to keep trying.

Support

Comments alone are not enough for your at-risk students. They also need you to take actions to support their specific needs. This may be something as basic as making sure they have the materials they need for class. Howard Johnston, a professor at the University of South Florida, tells a story about how schools treat students who forget to bring a pencil to class. He says, "Picture what happens when we are in a store, and we get to the checkout line and are ready to write a check, but we forgot a pen. The clerk doesn't say, 'You have to put your items back. I can't believe you didn't bring a pen with you to the store.' No, they give you something to write with. But in schools, we major on minors. We make a big deal over not having something to write with." His solution was to buy a box of small golf pencils and make them available to students. The students didn't particularly like the pencils, which helped them remember to bring one next time; but for the lesson at hand, they had the needed materials.

I would guess that you already help students who are struggling, possibly by offering to stay after school, come in before school, or meet with them during lunch. Unfortunately, the support is often optional, and the students who need assistance the most don't use it. Some don't believe they need the extra help, others don't believe that it will help, and still other students have valid reasons for not accepting your offer, such as not having transportation if they stay after school. It's important to push those students a little more, and refuse to allow them to *not* accept your help. If there is a logistical issue with getting help, work with the parents or family members and others in your school to solve that problem.

Time

Ultimately, inspiring students through your belief, encouragement, and support requires that you make a choice to invest your time in particular students. In fewer than five minutes per day, you can ask an extra question or say an extra positive comment several times during the day. And the time you spend providing extra help will maximize learning later. The important part is not the amount of time you spend; it is that you commit to doing these things consistently with the students.

As a final thought, holding all students to high expectations is one of the most challenging and rewarding things teachers do. As Annette Breaux's poem shows, your beliefs about your students are the most powerful lesson they learn from you.

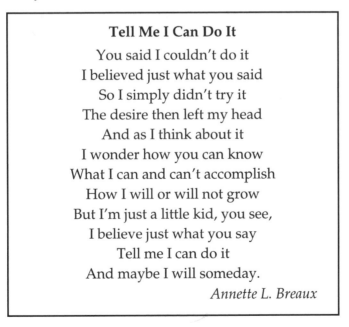

Tell Me I Can Do It

You said I couldn't do it
I believed just what you said
So I simply didn't try it
The desire then left my head
And as I think about it
I wonder how you can know
What I can and can't accomplish
How I will or will not grow
But I'm just a little kid, you see,
I believe just what you say
Tell me I can do it
And maybe I will someday.

Annette L. Breaux

Summary

- Remember that students will live up to (or down to) the expectations you set for them.
- Avoid *buts* about setting high expectations for each and every student.
- Be aware of the students who need more than others.
- Verbalize sincere belief in a student; it is a powerful motivator.
- Encourage—it is essential in education.
- Support your students in every way possible.
- Be available. A small amount of your time may make all the difference to a student.

If you would like more information...

The 90/90/90 Schools: A Case Study by D. B. Reeves, Advanced Learning Press. Full text available online at: http://www.makingstandards work. com/Downloads/AinA%20Ch19.pdf/.

Building Dreams: Helping Students Discover Their Potential by Mychal Wynn, Rising Sun Publishing.

Escalante: The Best Teacher in America by Jay Mathews, Henry Holt & Company.

Real Teachers, Real Challenges, Real Solutions: 25 Ways to Handle Challenges of the Classroom Effectively by Annette L. Breaux and Elizabeth Breaux, Eye On Education.

I

It's All About Me (the Value of Intrinsic Motivation)

I'm not going to write something particularly profound. I'm not saying anything that will have a huge impact on anyone's life. All I know is that I have spent much time searching for my motivation to succeed—anything at all that will drive me to do my best. What I have discovered is that motivation, whatever it may be, is absolutely not external; it comes from within. No one can provide motivation for you, it must come from your core, from your inner self. If it doesn't, then it's not motivation.

Author Unknown,
submitted by Jennifer G., age 15, New York
(http://www.motivateus.com/teens23a.htm)

Do you teach students who are intrinsically motivated? Intrinsic motivation comes from within. It's the sense of working toward something simply because we want to or because we see value in the accomplishment, and it is relatively easy to know when a student is intrinsically motivated. However, in schools, we focus much of our time and attention on extrinsic rewards such as points and prizes because they are so much easier; and they do motivate many students, particularly for the short term. Intrinsic motivation, however, seems to be harder for us. After all, how do you motivate someone to be self-motivated?

Indicators of a Students' Intrinsic Motivation

He or she:
Pursues the activity independently.
Enjoys the activity.
Doesn't want to stop working until finished.
Moves beyond the minimum expectations.
Doesn't care if there are rewards attached.

Foundational Elements

Intrinsic motivation has two foundational elements: People are more motivated when they value what they are doing and when they believe they have a chance for success. Although you can't provide either of these for your students, there are several key building blocks that support each.

Building Blocks for Value

First, students are more likely to be intrinsically motivated to learn if they value what they are asked to do. There are five building blocks to add value in your classroom.

VALUE Building Blocks

V	Variety
A	Attractiveness
L	Locus of Control
U	Utility
E	Enjoyment

Students are more likely to be motivated when they are not asked to do the same thing over and over again. What is your least favorite routine task? I hate paperwork. It doesn't matter if it's completing a travel form for reimbursement or organizing my tax records; I would rather do almost anything else. One day I realized that if I had to do paperwork every single day, over and over again, I would be miserable. That, however, is exactly how our students feel about some classes. There is an element of work involved in learning, but when students view learning as drudgery, they are less likely to be motivated to work.

Variety is enhanced when you make a lesson attractive. Attractiveness doesn't mean adding fluff to a lesson; it means integrating elements of curiosity and originality into your lessons.

Charlene Haviland, a teacher in Norfolk, Virginia, has developed lessons that incorporate this concept. She plans to use the Harry Potter books to teach science concepts. For a discussion on the flying broomsticks used in the game of Quidditch, Haviland said, "We can even go into Bernoulli's principle and explore how we can take that from flying on a broom to…how airplanes work…and why some fly better than others." (http://www.cnn.com/2005/EDUCATION/07/08/harry.potter.science.ap/index.html). I don't know about you, but I'd sign up for that class quicker than I would a standard class on aerodynamics.

The third building block, locus of control, refers to how students need to feel as though they have some control or choice in a given situation. This basically means that if Kinu feels trapped and like she is following orders, she is less likely to be motivated. Students are more apt to be intrinsically motivated if they have ownership in the learning—if they believe they are a part of the learning experience, rather than simply being told what to do.

Students also need to see the utility in learning. When I do workshops with teachers, I know they come into my session with one burning question: "How can I use this information immediately?" Adult learners are juggling so many demands, they prioritize activities and their attention based on how well something meets their immediate needs. Kids are similar, except they don't have the choice to leave. So often, we forget to show students why they need to know what we are teaching.

I was observing a student teacher when a student I'll call Darin asked, "Why do we need to learn this?" It clearly flustered her, particularly because I was there to observe her, and she snapped back, "Because I said so." You can imagine the look on Darin's face. Her answer ranks right up there with "Because we have to. It's on the test." Neither helps students understand why learning is important. Students are more engaged in learning when they see a useful connection to themselves.

The final block for building value is enjoyment. Students are more motivated when they find pleasure in what they are doing. During my first year of teaching, another teacher told me two things: "Don't smile before Christmas; and if your kids are enjoying the lesson, you're doing something wrong." Now I realize how unhappy she must have been. Although you need to have a classroom with structure and order, that may look different in various class-rooms. It is absolutely, positively okay to smile and have fun. Play games, make jokes, and do something different.

Building Blocks for Achieving Success

Students are also motivated when they believe they have a chance to be successful. And that belief is built on four additional building blocks: level of challenge, experiences, encouragement, and views about success.

First, the degree of alignment between the difficulty of an activity and a student's skill level is a major factor in self-motivation. Imagine that you enjoy riding a bicycle, and you have competed in a local race. You have the opportunity to race against Lance Armstrong. How do you feel? In that situation, there's plenty of opportunity for challenge, probably too much challenge! Or perhaps you love reading novels, but the only language you can read is Russian. How motivated will you be in a literature class? For optimal motivation, the activity should be challenging but in balance with your ability to perform. That's a struggle for many teachers; but that is the foundation of our jobs—starting where a student is, and moving him or her up to increasing levels of difficulty and providing appropriate scaffolding for learning at increasing levels.

Just as we've discussed in many other areas, a student's experiences are an important factor. I'm more likely to believe I can be successful in science if I've been successful in other science activities. On the other hand, if I've had multiple negative experiences reading poetry, I'm less likely to want to read poetry, because I don't think I can.

A third building block to feelings of success is the encouragement a student receives from others. Encouragement is "the process of facilitating the development of the person's inner resources and courage towards positive movement" (Dinkmeyer & Losoncy, 1980, p.16). The difference between encouragement and praise is simple; praise focuses on the performance of a student and is a form of extrinsic motivation; encouragement recognizes worth based on simple existence.

When you encourage, you accept students as they are, so they will accept themselves. You value and reinforce attempts and efforts, and help the student realize that mistakes are learning tools. Encouragement says, "Try, and try again. You can do it. Go in your own direction, at your own pace. I believe in you." Encouragement can be in the form of words, but you can also provide encouragement through a consistent, positive presence in your students' lives.

It's also important for students to read and learn about people who failed before they succeeded, because the final building block is a student's views about success and failure. Many students see failure as the end rather than as an opportunity to learn before trying again. How you define success and failure drives many of your beliefs about your own ability to succeed.

Do I Have to Choose Between Rewards and Intrinsic Motivation?

Although there are those who contend that extrinsic and intrinsic motivation are opposites and that teachers must choose one or the other, most teachers I meet take a middle-ground approach. They are opposites but not mutually exclusive. In a society that celebrates the value of rewards, a classroom that solely focuses on students' self-motivation is likely the exception, not the rule. However, we should strive to create a classroom environment that minimizes temporary, external rewards and encourages students to become self-motivated. It is possible. As Jennifer said, "No one can provide motivation for you, it must come from your core, from your inner self. If it doesn't, then it's not motivation."

Summary

- Build in a variety of teaching strategies and opportunities for assessment to keep students interested.
- Integrate elements of curiosity and novelty into your lessons.
- Help students feel ownership in an assignment; they are more likely to be motivated to complete it successfully.
- Demonstrate immediate uses for information for students to see the importance of acquiring the knowledge.
- Make learning fun—interest and energy cause motivation to increase.
- Ensure that students feel that success is within reach (with some effort) for every assignment that you give.
- Help students see that failure is often the only road that leads to success.
- Encourage students to believe in themselves.
- Minimize external rewards—instead, teach students to become more self-motivated.

If you would like more information...

This site discusses extrinsic and intrinsic motivation and how rewards may do harm: http://www.mentalhelp.net/psyhelp/chap4/chap4q.htm/.

This site contains information on how to capture children's natural intrinsic motivation in the classroom: http://seamonkey.ed.asu.edu/~jimbo/RIBARY_Folder/motivati.htm/.

Help Students Develop Self-Motivation: A Sourcebook for Parents and Teachers by Donald R. Grossnickle, National Association of Secondary School Principals.

The Encouragement Book: Becoming a Positive Person by Don Dinkmeyer and Lewis E. Losoncy, Prentice-Hall.

Punished by Rewards: The Trouble with Gold Stars, Incentive Plans, A's Praise and Other Bribes by Alfie Kohn, Houghton Mifflin.

J

Jump to Conclusions (Don't)

"Now will you tell me where we are?" asked Tock as he looked around the desolate island. "To be sure," said Canby; "you're on the Island of Conclusions. Make yourself at home. You're apt to be here for some time." "But how did we get here?" asked Milo, who was still a bit puzzled by being there at all. "You jumped, of course," explained Canby. "That's the way most everyone gets here. It's really quite simple; every time you decide something without having a good reason, you jump to Conclusions whether you like it or not. It's such an easy trip to make that I've been here hundreds of times." "But this is such an unpleasant-looking place," Milo remarked. "Yes, that's true," admitted Canby; "it does look much better from a distance."

from *The Phantom Tollbooth* by Norton Juster

Think About It...

Have you ever jumped to a conclusion about a student or a situation? Did you later discover that you made an incorrect assumption?

I had a student who was a constant challenge, and I taught him for 2½ years! Daniel came into my class with a reputation as a troublemaker, and in seventh grade he lived up to it. By the eighth grade, he was trying to improve, but he struggled to move beyond his past behavior patterns and others' preconceived notions of him. The turning point in our student-teacher relationship came when I discovered he had a talent for drawing, and I arranged for him to do some artwork for a special project. I was amazed at the turnaround from a completely negative attitude in my class the prior year to a positive attitude. In fact, if other students tried to misbehave, he would tell them to stop and pay attention. By the end of the year, he asked to be on the school newspaper in grade nine, in part because I was the sponsor. Based on his reputation, our guidance counselor was reluctant to approve his placement, but I went to bat for him; and he was the best student editorial cartoonist I ever worked with.

The year Daniel went to high school was the year I left my public school teaching job. I returned home one day and received a call from one of his relatives. Daniel had been expelled because he had a gun at school. I remember not asking, "Why did he do that?" but saying, "Tell me what else happened, because I don't think he would have brought a gun to school." His aunt was surprised at my response and said I was the only person who didn't assume his guilt. Another student brought the gun to school to shoot a third student, and Daniel took the gun away from the first student. When asked why he failed to bring this to the attention of an adult, he said he didn't trust any of the teachers enough to go to them with the gun because they wouldn't believe him, so he put it in his locker. When it was discovered, he was expelled.

I'm always reminded of Daniel's story when I read my favorite children's book, *The Phantom Tollbooth* by Norton Juster. During their journey, Milo, Tock, and the Humbug end up jumping to the Island of Conclusions, which turns out to be a less-than-pleasant place. I jumped to conclusions about Daniel based on our first day of class together, and it took me two years to move past that and build a strong relationship. I regret the wasted time, because I could have made so much more progress with him if I had started our teacher-student relationship differently.

Making the choice to *not* jump to conclusions is less about our students than it is about who we are as teachers. Annette Breaux's poem, *I'm Not the One You Think You Know,* provides a vivid student perspective of that point. I've come to learn that the heart of being an exceptional teacher involves moving beyond perceptions to see the real student.

Are you interested in meeting student needs? You have to probe deeper than surface actions to determine what is driving the student to take those actions. Do you want to solve a discipline problem? You have to deal with the cause, not the effect. Are you interested in being more successful with motivation? Then you have to suspend your prior beliefs about every kid who walks into your classroom and ask, "Who are you, who do you want to be, how can I help you get there?" The key is building positive, caring relationships with your students.

Discipline: Deal With the Cause, Not the Effect

Recently, I was waiting in the main office in a school when a young girl came in with a note to see the principal. She explained to the secretary that her band teacher sent her to the office because she forgot her flute. The secretary asked her why she forgot it, and she said she didn't really know—that she just did—for the third time. Intrigued by the conversation, I asked the student what she had to do in class when she forgot her flute, and she told me she had to copy definitions and read. I then asked, "So, you like doing that better than playing the flute?" She quickly replied, "Yes," then she caught herself and said, "No, not really." I asked, "Are you sure?" She seemed stunned, as if she had never thought about it or that no one had ever asked.

When I spoke with her teacher and shared our conversation, she also looked puzzled, then commented she had not thought about the reason for the behavior. She was frustrated with the student's poor behavior (not being prepared for class), and jumped to the conclusion that the student was being disrespectful. She had not taken the time to look for the cause behind the behavior. Isn't that typical? We are so busy and caught up in all the problems, we jump to the simplest or most expedient solution. Then, we deal with the effect (the misbehavior) rather than the cause.

Meeting Needs

Mr. Juarez told me about Mike, a student who showed no interest in reading. A discussion with other teachers brought up a variety of excuses—he's a boy, he doesn't know how to read, and so on. One day, Mr. Juarez told the class about a book he was reading in a graduate children's literature class and that he had read the same book when he was in elementary school. Mike was surprised that Mr. Juarez had ever read a book outside of those he read aloud to the class, and he expressed even more surprise that his teacher had a personal copy of the book. Mike said he didn't have any books. Mr. Juarez probed further and discovered there were no books in Mike's home. The only books available to Mike were those from the school.

By not jumping to conclusions, asking questions, and listening, he discovered that it wasn't that Mike couldn't read; he simply didn't know that reading was something you were supposed to do other than when you were told to do so in class. Mr. Juarez then decided to buy him a book to help him see that reading could be a great outside activity. After another conversation, Mike admitted to watching old western movies on television, so the teacher bought a book him a book about cowboys. He also met with Mike's grandmother, took them the public library to get a library card, and periodically asked Mike about reading. The result? Mike is now a solid grade-level reader who enjoys reading.

Personal Connection

A teacher in one of my graduate courses was frustrated by constant interruptions from a several her female students. No matter how busy Ms. Wolfe was, these students always demanded her attention. Most of the time, the questions were not urgent; and often they were somewhat trivial and repetitive. However, in response to an assignment in my class, she decided to implement a *stop-and-drop* policy: She would drop everything and give a student five minutes when he or she needed to talk, regardless of the circumstances.

Ms. Wolfe started this policy without telling her students. On the day she began, one of the girls caught her while en route to the copy machine and insisted on talking with her. For Ms. Wolfe, this first reminded her of all the other times that this girl had wanted to talk about trivial matters, but she remembered what she said she would do (*stop and drop*), so she walked the student back to her classroom to talk. The student confided that her boyfriend was pressuring her to have sex that afternoon after school, and she didn't know what to do. Ms. Wolfe talked with her about the importance of not rushing into a decision, not making any decision based on pressure, and recommended that she talk to her parents. That night, the mother called to thank her for taking the time to help her daughter. The mother was stunned—she had no idea that her daughter was even thinking of this—and she appreciated that the teacher helped the student to discuss it with her parents and make a different decision.

Motivate through Personal Relationships

My former professor, Dr. John Van Hoose, told of an experience with a school in Ohio. The faculty identified 40 struggling students who consistently underachieved and were in and out of the office for behavioral issues. Twenty teachers volunteered to work with them, and the program was organized simply. The teacher met with his or her two students for five minutes at the beginning of the day and five minutes at the end of the day. At the start of the day, the teacher asked, "How was your evening? Did you finish your homework last night? Do you have everything you need for school today?" At the end of the day, the teacher asked, "How was your day today? Do you have everything you need to take home to study? Is there anything going on I need to know about?" At the end of the first year, almost every student successfully completed the school year. A small number were suspended, but most of the students had improved behaviorally and academically.

It's so easy to jump to that island of conclusions. You have a test score; you have a record of discipline issues; you have an attitude that comes through everyday in your class. Some of your kids may completely live up to that reputation. But other students could shine *if* the right person takes the time to listen, care, and help. If you teach 120 students per day, you may be saying, "I don't have time to build a personal relationship with 120 students." I agree.

But look at what the school did; they focused on the students who needed them the most, and put extra effort there. You have some students with plenty of support at home who will be fine with the standard attention you pay to all students. But you also have a small number of students who need more attention; and it doesn't have to be hard. I saw a bulletin board in an elementary school teacher's lounge that said kids need the most love when they least deserve it. I think this is so true. They actually need the most love, patience, or understanding when they least deserve it and usually when they don't deserve it at all!

One teacher made the decision to do this with Jorge. He was disengaged during class, preferring to slink into his seat and be ignored. Every time he came to class, the teacher asked him if he had his homework, how his day was going, and if he understood the content of the lesson (pretty standard questions, you might be thinking). By the end of the year, Jorge was bringing his homework to class, volunteering to answer questions, and improving his grades. His perspective on the situation? "I started doing my homework so my teacher wouldn't bug me; but then I realized I could do it, so then I wanted to." It would have been easy for this teacher to simply ignore Jorge, assuming that he just wasn't a good student. After all, that's how jumping to conclusions are—easy. But, as Norton Juster tells us in *The Phantom Tollbooth*, "You can never jump away from Conclusions. Getting back is not so easy. That's why we're so terribly crowded here."

The crowd is on the Island of Conclusions—we have all jumped to conclusions that we have later regretted. But, we can make the choice today to limit our trips there. We can choose to wait, ask questions, and try to understand each student before we make a judgment call. After making too many trips to that island, I've decided to follow Milo's advice: "…from now on I'm going to have a very good reason before I make up my mind about anything. You can lose too much time jumping to Conclusions."

Summary

- Make a conscious choice to not jump to conclusions.
- Find the true cause of someone's misbehavior or lack of effort. Don't just assume a student is simply being disrespectful. Take the time to find out what a student needs (or what is lacking at home).
- Build some sort of personal connection with every student. You may be the one person they feel like they can talk to.
- Give students patience and understanding when they don't seem to deserve it at all, which is when they actually need it the most.

If you would like more information…

The Compassionate Classroom: Relationship Based Teaching and Learning by Sura Hart and Victoria Kindle Hodson, PuddleDancer Press.

Connecting With Students by Allen N. Mendler, ASCD.

Keys to Evaluation:
Grading and Motivation

I think the big mistake in schools is trying to teach children anything, and by using fear as the basic motivation. Fear of getting failing grades, fear of not staying with your class, etc. Interest can produce learning on a scale compared to fear as a nuclear explosion to a firecracker.

Stanley Kubrick

Think About It...

Do your students work harder in your class to make a better grade?

The notion of evaluation, assessment, and grading is enough to fill an entire book! In this chapter, I'm going to narrow the focus to providing guidelines for evaluating learning and address how grading and evaluation impact students' motivation.

Evaluation is the process of making a decision about the degree to which students understand a concept. We make those decisions using informal data, such as our observations of students' responses during a discussion, and using formal data, such as students' performance on a test or on a project.

And in almost every school, grades and standardized test scores are the most visible symbols of evaluation.

When I started teaching elementary and junior high school, evaluating students was a struggle. I was never sure if I was doing it correctly or if there was one correct way to evaluate and grade. Advice from colleagues was pretty simple: Be able to back up anything you put down as a grade and save everything. I kept a file of student folders, which included every paper or test that was graded. I mainly used them if a parent or a student questioned a grade. As I look back on that experience, I see how focused I was on the wrong thing, particularly because those files were a treasure chest of information with far more potent uses.

During that period, I looked on grading as having to prove that my opinion was correct. I felt as though I was on the defensive, and as a result, grading was my least favorite task. After I started teaching remedial students, for whom grades seemed to matter in a different way, I shifted my focus. I thought about why I graded something, how I graded it, and lastly, how I could explain it to my students and parents. And my evaluation of students and the grading process became more authentic and valuable to me and my students.

Purpose of Evaluating and Grading

What is your purpose for grading a particular assignment? Are you setting a benchmark to see which of your students have met a standard? Or are you evaluating their progress, so you can make decisions about your future instruction? One of my problems the first year of teaching was that I didn't have a good answer to that question. In fact, if you asked me why I was grading something, my answer would have been, "So I can have enough grades for the report card." I didn't understand that evaluating students is more than grades, and that it is important to think about my purpose.

There are several purposes of evaluation. Schools use evaluation to make decisions about placements, particularly in ability-leveled classes or promotion to the next grade level. The process of moving students to higher levels requires some type of evaluative judgment.

Teachers also use evaluative data to group students and plan for instruction tailored to specific needs. This is one of the most important uses of evaluation. If you collect information about a student, but don't use it to plan what to teach next (or what to reteach), what use is it? Closely linked to this purpose is the notion of using evaluative data to provide feedback to students, so they can improve. Both purposes require that you plan the type of assessment used to ensure you gain the specific information you need to make decisions.

Grades as Extrinsic Motivators

A final use of grades is to externally motivate students. Some students respond well to this form of motivation; grades are just a higher-stakes version of receiving a pizza for reading books. You simply can't get away from the fact that grades provide external pressure on students. Some thrive in this situation; others suffer. Parents and/or family members may complicate the situation if they value the grades differently or more than the student.

Most of the teachers I know use some form of grades as motivation. The most common activity I see is giving students extra points. Many parents give additional rewards, such as money, if students earn certain grades. This can be positive, but it also can undermine a student's intrinsic motivation, so balance is important. Grades are a part of our society, and students need to learn to deal with them. However, an overemphasis on grades will undermine learning.

I found this comment by Ronald Reagan to be funny, yet sad. *"But there are advantages to being elected President. The day after I was elected, I had my high school grades classified Top Secret."* How many students wish their grades could be classified? And what does that tell us as teachers? At a minimum, it reminds us that students should be allowed some privacy with their grades. Many teachers post students' tests with grades on a bulletin board. Although I encourage the posting of student work, be cautious when posting grades on public displays of work, because this can have long-term, detrimental effects on your students.

How to Grade

Once you know why you want to grade something, you can determine the format that best meets that purpose. For example, if you simply want to use grades to place students into skill-based groups, you need to use some form of test or product that specifically shows you what a student does and does not know. You can't group students for additional math instruction on fractions if your test only included two questions about fractions. Or, if you want to provide feedback on students' use of grammar in writing, a test in which they underline subjects and verbs does not provide you the best information.

You can use a variety of methods to evaluate: multiple choice or other *pick-an-answer* questions, short-answer questions, essay questions, projects, oral reports, teacher observations, and even student self-assessments. There are multiple resources available to you to help you decide what to use. Just make sure that it provides you the information you need to match your purpose.

Rubrics

A popular tool for evaluation is a rubric, which is a set of guidelines that define levels of quality. Rubrics can be used with any projects or assignments and are a helpful tool for communicating expectations.

Creating Rubrics

Identify purpose of rubric
Identify criteria
Determine levels of assessment
Describe levels

Cindy Linn, a teacher in Fairfax County, Virginia, encourages her students to read at home and uses a rubric to give students and parents a clear set of expectations (see example).

Communicating About Evaluation

I believe it is critical to have a clear explanation for your philosophy and/or policy about grading. If homework counts, students and parents need to know that.

The last thing you want to hear from a student or a parent is, "If I had just known…." One of the school districts I work with requires all teachers to provide a written grading policy. They don't dictate the terms of the policy; they believe teachers should have that choice. However, all teachers must have a written explanation of what and how they grade, and provide reminders to students of the policies.

Cindy Linn's Rubric

	Awesome (4)	Bravo (3)	Catching On (2)	Did not get it (1)
Discussions	• Read and made notes (post-its, annotations, questions) • Intellectually engaged and enthusiastically ready for the discussion • Contributes original and insightful comments.	• Read and able to participate with some notes • Intellectually prepared, ready to think about the book and related ideas. • Contributes appropriate ideas and observations with some insights.	• Completed most of the reading • Has book and/or bookmark • Somewhat prepared intellectually • Contributes only when called upon but ideas are appropriate	• Did not complete the reading; unable to participate. • Does not have book or bookmark • Not intellectually prepared to enter into serious discussion
Responses	• Read and made notes (post-its, annotations, and questions) • Response to the prompt shows originality and insight • Excellent composition, written expression and mechanics	• Read and has a few post-it notes. • Responds to the prompt with appropriate ideas and observations and some insights • Well done composition, written expression and/or mechanics	• Completed most of the reading • Has book and/or bookmark Response to the prompt is minimal • Weak composition, written	• Did not complete the reading; unable to participate. • No book or bookmark • Not intellectually prepared to enter into serious discussion • Weak composition, written expression and mechanics
Goals	• Surpassed reading page/time goal, clearly ready to discuss and/or write about the book. • Articulates progress toward reading skill goal.	• Reached reading page/time goal, ready to discuss or write about the book. • Making progress toward reading skill goal.	• Close to reading page/time goal • Missing bookmark or book. • Making some progress toward reading skill goal.	• Missing bookmark and book • Little or no attempt to work on reading skill goal

www.teacherleaders.org/misc/cindy/Reading_Ltr_Parents.doc

The Pitfalls of Grading

In many cases, grades have become a status symbol, rather than a measure of learning. I talk to teachers who are pressured to give a student a higher grade. In states that provide scholarships based on a student's high school grade point average (GPA), there is intense pressure by parents to ensure their son or daughter gets the scholarship "I paid for." The result is pressure on teachers to inflate grades so students have a higher GPA. The issue is not just social status; it's thousands of dollars on the line for that student and family.

My Current Grading Policy

Although I struggle less with grades now than I did as a first year teacher, I can't tell you that grading is easy for me. Graduate students are entirely different creatures when it comes to grades. Every semester, I have at least one discussion with a student who is upset over a grade, typically because he or she made a B instead of an A! If I had my choice, I'd teach in a situation with no grades. To the extent that I can, I deemphasize grades with my students.

My students receive clear guidelines and a detailed rubric for all projects, which count more than tests. Although I use a standard grading scale for exams, my grading scale is adapted for projects: A, B, and Not Yet (NY). If a student receives a NY, we meet and discuss what is needed for revision. The student has a week to revise the work up to a B. In one case, a student chose not to revise work and received the lower grade she earned. Overall, my students like the policy, because it focuses on progress and understanding, rather than punishment. It works for me, but I have colleagues who say it would never work for them.

That's exactly why I am not giving you a lockstep method for grading. Although grading is a public decision, because the results are always shared with at least one other person, I believe that decisions about grading are intensely personal—a reflection of who you are and what you believe about learning. I won't give you a formula that tells you exactly what to use each time you need to evaluate your students. What I can tell you is that there are four guidelines to help you decide how to grade.

Grading Guidelines

1. Use a variety of assessments; one size does not fit all.

2. Make sure the type of assessment matches your purpose.

3. Clearly explain to your students what you are evaluating and the purpose of the evaluation.

4. Create and provide your students (when appropriate) with clear guidelines for your evaluation.

The ultimate question about grading is this: Do you and your students respond to grades out of fear? Stanley Kubrick's perspective, that schools use fear to motivate, is a strong view. Unfortunately for some students, his comments are all too real. We are spending this entire book talking about creating a motivating classroom environment, but fear will undermine it quicker than almost anything else you can do. Plan evaluation with a focus on improvement, and watch your students grow.

Summary

- Evaluation is the process of making a judgment about the degree to which students understand a concept.
- Determine your purpose for grading an assignment before even giving it to students.
- Don't undermine learning with an overemphasis on grades.
- Determine which format of evaluation will best assess the specific knowledge you are looking for, and try to vary the methods you use.
- Use rubrics as a helpful tool for communicating clear expectations.
- Communicate a clear homework and grading policy to students and parents.
- Provide clear rubrics or guidelines on the criteria you will be grading before making an assignment whenever possible.
- Focus on using grades as a temporary measure of progress or understanding rather than a permanent punishment that cannot be improved.

If you would like more information...

This site provides teachers with rubrics to use in the classroom: http://rubistar.4teachers.org/index.php/.

Great Performances: Creating Classroom-Based Assessment Tasks by Larry Lewin and Betty Jean Shoemaker, ASCD.

Transforming Classroom Grading by Robert J. Marzano, ASCD.

Wad-ja-Get by Howard Kirschenbaum.

L

Literacy

Literacy arouses hopes, not only in society as a whole but also in the individual who is striving for fulfillment, happiness and personal benefit by learning how to read and write. Literacy...means far more than learning how to read and write...The aim is to transmit...knowledge and promote social participation.

United Nations Educational Scientific
and Cultural Organization Institute for Education,
Hamburg, Germany

The opening quotation from the United Nations Educational Scientific and Cultural Organization (UNESCO) sets a context for our discussion of literacy. I work with teachers who tell me that literacy is something only *reading teachers* should deal with. But everyone can teach the use of reading and writing for understanding and communication, skills that encompass all areas of instruction.

Think About It...

How has a student's lack of literacy skills impacted his or her learning in your classroom?

81

Literacy for All Subjects

I present a variety of workshops for teachers, particularly on content literacy or literacy across the curriculum. Invariably, someone will say, "I don't teach reading and writing. I teach math or music (or something other than English/language arts)." The reality is that everyone is a literacy teacher. I'm not asking you to stop your science lesson and teach reading or writing for 10 minutes. Literacy is the key that unlocks the understanding of your content, however, and you need to teach your students how to use that key in your content area.

Working With Vocabulary

Do you have vocabulary words you want students to learn? I was in a social studies classroom in which the teacher was presenting geography terms such as equator, latitude, and longitude. She drew a circle on the board to illustrate Earth then she wrote the word "equator" across the center. The word "latitude" was also written horizontally from west to east where the latitude lines went across the Earth. Finally, the word "longitude" was written vertically from north to south to clearly illustrate her point, rather than simply writing the words beside the diagram (see the illustration). This also assisted students in taking clear notes they could study at home.

Equator

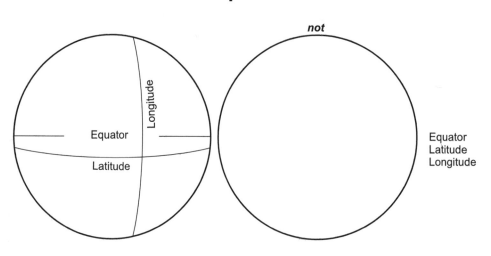

Another way to make vocabulary more memorable is to have students develop ways to help them remember the meaning of the word. My students enjoyed creating concrete poems for new words, and posting them helped everyone learn, such as in the Concrete Poem picture (below). We also used acrostics as memory tools, and as you can tell from this book, I still use them to help organize information in an easy format.

Concrete Poem

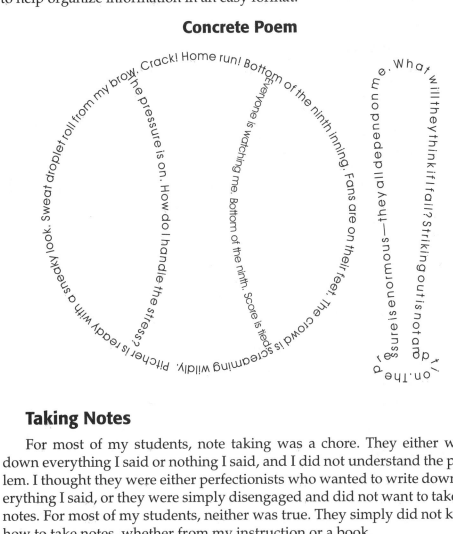

Taking Notes

For most of my students, note taking was a chore. They either wrote down everything I said or nothing I said, and I did not understand the problem. I thought they were either perfectionists who wanted to write down everything I said, or they were simply disengaged and did not want to take the notes. For most of my students, neither was true. They simply did not know how to take notes, whether from my instruction or a book.

I began to teach them to use a simple note taking format with two columns. On the left side, I provided an outline of the main topics I would teach, and students took notes about each point on the right. For more structure, I sometimes put the number of points they should have on the right side. For example, when I taught the regions of North Carolina, the right side had three bullets so they knew to listen for three regions. I have seen teachers use a variety of other formats, such as Cornell notes, but one of the most effective is a variation of what I used in my own classroom. It adds a third column to the two I described, one column for reminders, which allows students to come up with their own way to remember the content. This can be a picture or a word—anything that will jog their memories about the notes. Again, the point is to give them hooks on which to hang their knowledge.

Using the Textbook

Textbooks are difficult for many students. When I worked as a consultant with a textbook company, I learned the importance of teaching students how to use their textbooks. Of course, there are the basic organizing structures such as the table of contents, index, or glossary; but there is so much more. Many students at all grade levels may not know that chapter subheadings form an outline or that bold-faced words are important new terms that are likely defined in the sentence, glossary, and possibly even in the margin. Textbook publishers add extra study aids to assist students in understanding the content, but often our students don't realize they are there or know how to use them. Therefore, it is important to teach your students how to use your specific textbook.

One way is to simply talk students through the book: "Now this year we're using a new textbook in my class. And one of the things I did was sit down and look through it and see what is available to help me use the textbook most effectively. So for example, you will see three questions at the start of a chapter. Chances are those questions are also going to be on the test at the end." And just walk them through the other key elements in the book. Another option is to do a scavenger hunt, and let your students work in groups to discover those study helps together.

Reading and Responding

Reading some form of text material and responding to it is a pretty standard activity in most classrooms. Too often, students read silently, then answer questions. As an alternative, my undergraduate students read a chapter of their textbook and place at least three Post-it notes throughout the selection. On each one, they can write a comment or a question about what they have read. That becomes the basis for our discussion in class. Periodically, I have them take the Post-it notes out of the book, stick them on a piece of paper, add their name, and then I take it up for a pop quiz grade.

Kendra Alston uses a countdown method with her students. She holds up a colorful card to "count down" from five. See the Countdown for Reading for an example.

Countdown for Reading

5	Golden lines (interesting stories, phrases, etc. from the text)
4	New vocabulary terms and your own personal definition
3	Key points from the text
2	Your own ideas about the subject
1	Question you still have

Doing Research

Another important aspect of literacy is the ability to research a topic. Chad Maguire, a math teacher, asks his students to research and write about a famous mathematician. After giving students an overview of the project and sharing brief biographies of mathematicians, he randomly draws students' names, and they hold a draft similar to a professional sports draft to select their subjects. The finished report must include standard information about the person, but students also present the information in a creative way, such as role-playing the mathematician or creating a game. As a final incentive, students earn bonus points based on the number of things they have in common with the person they research.

Tracie Clinton begins the research process with her third graders. She explains, I give each of my students a person to research, a 2-liter bottle, a foam head, and two wiggly eyes. The students create the person they research with the items I provide. They add clothing and accessories. We also use class time to create individual PowerPoint presentations of their person. We invite parents and our principal to our classroom to view their projects in which they work so hard on. The bottle people are also displayed in the media center for everyone to see." When students research, write about, and present topics, content learning is enhanced.

Think About It...

If you teach a subject other than English/language arts, which of the areas described above is an issue with your students? Do you need to focus on research? Note taking? Vocabulary?

Real-Life Reading and Writing

When you consider literacy instruction, don't forget to include a focus on real-life examples of reading and writing. Students who may not be thrilled about reading a literary selection might be more interested in reading a comic book or the newspaper. My first year teaching at-risk students, I asked my principal if we could use *USA Today* for reading. My students didn't like carrying a different textbook, because other students knew if you carried the green book that meant you were in the "dumb" class. At that time, *USA Today* was new, and it was the only newspaper to print in color. My kids were excited to read "real stuff."

Lennie was one of my most reluctant readers. He did not see the value of reading until he turned 15 and needed to take the test to get his driver's permit. He discovered he needed to be able to study the manual to pass the test, so he asked me to teach him how to read the driver's manual. I agreed, and that evolved into some effective lessons with all students. I talk to many teachers who don't want to use anything other than a textbook, but that limits you and your students. Online sources, magazines, newspapers, and even comic books can supplement and enhance your instruction.

Just as students are more motivated to read for authentic purposes, they prefer writing for authentic purposes. Think of your students right now. Would they rather write a paragraph or a commercial, poem, or theme song? *USA Today* regularly profiles teachers through their All-USA Teacher Team. Mark Mueller, a member of the 2004 team, notes, "I'm interested in all forms of communication—essays, scripts, stories, plays, websites, debates, advertising. The underlying skill is the ability to express ideas well. Writing, communication, and logical thought are the keys to opening up their future." Through authentic reading and writing, students learn to prepare for the future.

No matter what subject or grade level you teach, literacy is a foundational skill for every student. And, as the opening quotation reminds us, literacy provides hope for the future for each of your students.

Summary

- Everyone is a literacy teacher!
- Literacy skills unlock the understanding of your content.
- Visual representations of concepts or vocabulary can make otherwise abstract concepts concrete to some students.

- Taking notes is a skill which must be taught so that students can organize a wealth of information.
- Students need to be shown how to use all the helpful features of their textbook.
- Students may respond to text when you teach using multiple creative ways.
- Authentic exploration and research is an important literacy skill to incorporate into all content areas.
- There should be frequent opportunities for real-life reading and writing (applicable and relevant to their lives).

If you would like more information...

These sites contain information on teaching literacy skills: http://www. infolit.org/ and http://www.reading.org/.

Literacy Strategies: Resources for Beginning Teachers, 1–6 by Terry Norton and Betty Lou Jackson Land, Prentice Hall.

Strategies That Work: Teaching Comprehension to Enhance Understanding by Stephanie Harvey and Anne Goudvis, Stenhouse Publishers.

Subjects Matter: Every Teacher's Guide to Content-Area Reading by Harvey Daniels and Steven Zemelman, Heinemann.

Tools For Teaching Content Literacy by Dr. Janet Allen, Stenhouse Publishers.

M

Myths of Motivation

Teachers open the door, but you must enter by yourself.

Chinese proverb

\multicolumn{2}{c}{**Think About It...**}	
\multicolumn{3}{l}{From your experience, which of the following statements are true or false?}		
True	**False**	**Statement**
		I teach at least one student who is not motivated.
		I know that I can motivate the students in my class.
		There are students in my class that I simply cannot motivate.

When I talk with teachers, I hear many misconceptions about motivation, so it's important to clarify and understand some of the major myths about student motivation.

Four Myths About Motivation

> The student just is not motivated.
> You can motivate someone.
> You cannot motivate someone.
> You cannot unmotivate someone.

Myth One: The Student Just Is Not Motivated

Have you ever said this about a student? I know I did when I was teaching—usually when nothing I did worked with a particular student. But this is never true; we are all motivated by something. When you say this, chances that you really mean that your student is not motivated by what you want or expect.

Let me explain using two examples. Philip is the class clown who never misses an opportunity to crack a joke. He doesn't do his homework, and any time you ask him to respond in class, he turns it into an opportunity to perform a comedy routine. From your perspective, he is just a cutup who draws other students away from learning. You have tried to deal with this in a couple of ways, including referring him to the office for misbehavior. You noticed, however, that the next day at lunch, he was entertaining his classmates with the story of his visit to the office. Finally, out of desperation, you have decided not to call on Philip anymore, to limit his opportunities to act up in class.

Tiffani, however, is quiet and doesn't volunteer to answer questions. You always make an effort to include her in the class discussion, even though she never gives more than a one-word answer. When you ask her, even privately, if she needs help, her answer is always "No, I'm fine." Her grades and classroom performance indicate that she has potential to learn, but her lack of response to your offer of help is hindering her from reaching her full potential. Finally, you told her you are calling her parents in to talk about her work, and she bursts into tears. Despite your reassurances that you are not calling to complain, she can't stop crying.

In each of these cases, it's easy to accept the myth the students aren't motivated; on the surface, they don't seem care. But, the students are strongly motivated by two powerful emotions: pleasure and pain. Philip craves attention and wants to be popular. His parents are divorced; and at lunch with his friends who laugh at his jokes, he feels good because he temporarily forgets that his parents argue all the time.

Tiffani, on the other hand, is reacting from fear. She has five brothers and sisters at home, and her parents have said that children should be seen and not heard. Her oldest brother dropped out of school, robbed a convenience store and is in prison. Her sister was suspended from school so often that she also decided to drop out of school. Her parents were so angry, they made her live with an aunt and uncle in another state. Tiffany overheard her parents tell her grandmother, "Tiffani is the good one because she is quiet and doesn't cause problems. At least she doesn't get into trouble at school." Tiffani is scared that if her teacher calls home, her parents will think she is just like her older brother and sister.

In each case, the student is motivated—just not by you or your classroom. This happens far too often. To combat the myth of students just aren't motivated, learn as much as you can about your students and their interests.

Myth Two: You Can Motivate Someone

This is a double-edged sword. It's true that you can motivate someone to perform a particular action (think of trained seals), but you aren't truly motivating him or her for any length of time. If the stakes are high enough, and if you use the right rewards or punishment, even the most resistant person will conform long enough to get the reward or avoid the punishment. But, to motivate the student to continue, you would have to ratchet up the stakes.

I have seen this happen with a popular reading incentive program. Students earn points by passing a test showing they read the book. Then, students cash in their points for rewards. This sounds pretty good (I know I like the rewards I can earn with my frequent flier points), but it can take a negative turn. I've been in schools where the prizes are pencils, or bookmarks, or books; but as students get older, they want or need more and better prizes to keep reading. The prizes become electronic games or CDs. I was appalled to read a news story praising an area high school for their innovative reading program. The school wanted to encourage reading, so it purchased the incentive program; and to motivate their students, they gave away a car!

You've probably seen the same thing in terms of using punishment as a motivator. Eric constantly misbehaved in my class, and he quickly progressed through all the negative consequences in my behavior plan. Isolating him didn't work, so I tried lunch detention. When that didn't work, we used in-school suspension. Of course, the next time, that didn't work, so we tried out-of-school suspension. By the end of the first nine weeks, I realized that I had already used every single negative consequence in my discipline plan along with several others that I tried just in case. I believed I could motivate him (myth two), but because I never found the real reasons for his behavior, I was only able to get short-term results.

Myth Three: You Cannot Motivate Someone

This is the other edge of that sword. As I just discussed, you can motivate actions for the short term, but let's take a long-term view here. Although you cannot make someone else be motivated, you can set up an environment or situation where they are more likely to be motivated.

Kendra Alston, Academic Facilitator at Kennedy Middle School, shared a lesson she learned during a high school social studies class. She wasn't excited to study the 1920s and 1930s, but her teacher, Mr. Baldwin told them he was giving a *show me what you know* final exam. "He didn't care how you showed it, as long as you showed what you know. Things flashed before my eyes, but I was into theatre. So I researched the vaudeville circuit at time and found Bessie Smith in theatre. She was a blues singer who sang in speakeasies; and I learned about the 20s and 30s through her eyes. On day of the exam, I came in singing, stayed in character (others did essays, etc.). He asked questions and I answered based on what Bessie Smith would have said. It's the only way I got through it."

This is a perfect example of a teacher creating an opportunity for a student to be motivated about learning. Rather than learning for the purpose of answering a question on a test, she channeled her interests into learning the content. And the lesson still resonates with her more than 15 years later. "What I would say about motivation is to find what your students love to teach them." She applies this lesson now with her own students:

> When you are introducing something they aren't into, you have to connect. Michael was in my 4th-grade class. His mom told me, "he hates to write, I know this year he has to, I'm worried about the test [state writing test]." All I have to do is know what they love, and he loved sports. So, I start with prewriting. One day, I had them bring something from home; I didn't tell them why to bring it in (the assignment would be to make an inanimate item talk). He brought in a soccer ball, and I asked him why it was his favorite item. He immediately told me about playing soccer, and that he won a championship. I started writing down what he said, and then I asked him to write about it. He told me all about the game he won, how his dad looked when he kicked for goal, etc. I knew everything because he loved it. So then, every time we had a topic, Michael would write about something sports related. He had to take his strength, sports, to help out in writing.

The myth that you cannot motivate someone is only partially true. The entire purpose of this book is to provide you with specific strategies that create an environment in which your students are more likely to be motivated. You cannot motivate them, but if you make specific efforts to connect with your students, they will respond.

Myth Four: You Cannot Unmotivate Someone

This is also not true. James, the son of a friend, loved to read. His parents read to him from infancy, and I provided a regular supply of books. By the time he was in the second grade, he was reading far above grade level. His teacher said she needed to work with those who did not know how to read, so she put him on a computer reading program every day. Reading changed for him because he was limited to reading books on an approved list. He was frustrated because some of the books he wanted to read were not on the list, and he was no longer allowed to choose his own books. Also, the value of reading was limited. Previously, he read for the pure joy of discovery and the discussions he could have with other people about what he had read. Unfortunately, his teacher didn't let him talk to the other students about books; his task was to take a test about the book instead.

Kendra had a similar situation as a student. When she was in the third grade, she loved to write; she still does. During each of the first two days, the teacher asked students to write about a certain topic. Although she always loved to write and everyone else was writing, she just sat in her desk—upset because she had always loved to write. On the second day, Kendra again wrote nothing, thinking, "I was the dumbest thing in the world."

The teacher called her parents and informed them that Kendra had a *U* in writing. During the subsequent parent conference, her mother asked, "What did you ask her to write?" On the first day of school, the teacher told the class to "write about time you had a sleep over," and on the second day, students had to write about the "time you had fight with a brother or sister." Kendra's mother explained that Kendra had never been on a sleep over, because she and her husband did not allow that until junior high. Also, Kendra was an only child. "How can you ask her to write about something she doesn't know about?" Despite a request from her parents to let her write about something she knew or was interested in, the teacher refused.

In each of the situations, a teacher was able to unmotivate a student. Whether it's because of intentional efforts, or simply a lack of understanding, our actions can have a negative effect on a student's motivation. I truly believe that we should treat each student in a way that nourishes a sense of hope for the future. But at a minimum, we should follow the same rule as physicians and *first, do no harm.* Betsy Rogers, 2003 National Teacher of the Year, posted a quote on her online blog (http://blogs.edweek.org/teachers/brogers/) that encapsulates this for me. She notes, "Rick Stiggins states as educators, our motto should be 'Do not deprive of hope.'" When we buy into some of these myths, that's what we do; we deprive our students of hope.

Think About It...

Go back to the statements at the beginning of the chapter. Which one(s) do you think are true now?

Summary

- All students are motivated—you just have to figure out what causes them to react. Get to know their background and interests.
- True motivation isn't accomplishment by short-term rewords or punishments.
- You have the power to establish an environment and atmosphere to develop internal motivation of your students.
- Unfortunately, you also have the power to negatively effect a student's motivation. So choose your words and actions carefully!

If you would like more information...

This site provides many tips on motivating your students: http://teaching.berkeley.edu/bgd/motivate.html/.

Creating Highly Motivating Classrooms for All Students: A Schoolwide Approach to Powerful Teaching with Diverse Learners by Margery B. Ginsberg, Raymond J. Wlodkowski, Jossey-Bass.

Motivating Your Students: Before You Can Teach Them, You Have to Reach Them by Hanoch McCarty and Frank Siccone, Allyn and Bacon.

Motivation to Learn: Integrating Theory and Practice, 4th edition by Deborah Stipek, Allyn and Bacon.

N

Never Give Permission

Never give anyone permission to take away your chance for success.

Sam Myers, Sumter 17 School District

Ronita, one of my former students, generally struggled in class. One day, after much hard work and studying, she made an A on a project. I was so proud of her but was stunned at her response. First, she said she was "lucky." After I assured her that wasn't true, she thanked me for "giving" her an A. She just didn't get it; the A it wasn't because of any outside force (luck or me), it was her; her efforts had earned the grade.

Unfortunately, many students are like Ronita. They don't have a strong internal locus of control—an inner confidence that they have choices and are in control of their behavior. When comparing people who are successful in an area of life (business, sports, etc.), they have one thing in common: Each had a clear vision for their life and a strong belief that they could achieve their dreams, that they were in control of their own destiny.

Compare that to people who find themselves simply existing from day to day. At some point, they look back at their life and ask, "How did I end up here? When I was young, I dreamed of [insert example]." As you talk to them, they will say things such as, "I wanted to be a musician, but someone else won the competition." "I tried to get the promotion, but my boss doesn't like me." "I could have been a pro athlete, but no one gave me a chance." You can tell from the language; it's always about someone or something else. They view control as external, or outside themselves. It's always about other people or circumstances. There are many societal elements that encourage this attitude. Did you get in a fight? The other person started it, so you didn't have a choice. Did you miss out on a promotion? The system is unfair. Did you commit a crime? It was because you watch television. The excuses mentality undermines having an internal sense of control.

Our focus in this chapter is self-empowerment. It is about encouraging students to believe in themselves and to do that by telling students two things:

1. You need to have a dream or vision that is the basis for your everyday choices and decisions.

2. Whether you succeed or fail is up to you. Period.

Tapping into an internal sense of choice and control is one of the hardest things for us to do, even as adults. Is it any wonder that students struggle with it? As a teacher, you cannot make someone believe in herself or himself; but you can provide structures, activities, and modeling to facilitate those positive beliefs.

Structures

One of the most basic ways to encourage the internal sense of control is to simply not allow any expressions of a lack of control. I never allowed students to use the phrase "I can't" in my classroom. You may choose not to try or you may not want to or you may not be there yet, but saying you can't simply isn't an option. It took several weeks, but the students really bought into it. Again, I am unable to make you believe in yourself, but I refuse to reinforce your lack of belief.

Belief building is critical. I have a strong belief that I can tackle any challenge. A friend asked me how I became so confident; where or when did I get my belief that I could achieve my dreams? My belief in myself is built on a strong base of memories. First, I have countless memories of people who believed in me and shared that belief with me. My parents, my grandparents, former teachers, friends—the list is long. Their encouragement helped me learn to believe in myself, even when I wasn't successful with a project. Second, based on their support, many times I persisted through failure until I succeeded. The memories of those successes give me the strength to attempt the next challenge.

Your students need the same memories. They will remember the times you show them you believe in them. Students remember the smiles, the kind words, and the opportunity and encouragement to try again when they fail.

But they sometimes forget the successes they achieve. When my students are struggling with an assignment, I'm quick to remind them of the other times when a project seemed difficult but was finished successfully. That's the essence of belief building; helping students realize their own potential.

Activities

Seeing Choices

For my students, that lack of an internal sense of control came out in one specific way; many of them never took responsibility for their own actions. If Mitch forgot his homework, it was his mother's fault for not reminding him. If Laura didn't turn in her project, I forgot to remind her. When two of my students got in a fight, you can imagine what happened. I asked Samantha why she hit Natasha and she said, "Because she hit me."

That simple response reflects a lack of a sense of control. Samantha is saying she had no choice—it was simply a reflex, and she had nothing to do with it. I turned that into a teaching tool. I used a graphic organizer to revisit the incident with everyone, broadening the issue for all students by asking "What would you do if you had the chance to fight someone?"

Now, play out the decisions—coax them into laying them out. Samantha had multiple choices. First, she could have hit Natalie back (the choice she made). Next, she could have told the teacher. Any others? She could have walked away and done nothing. So, let's say those are the three options she comes up with. Next, walk through the consequences as in the Decision Table.

Decision Table

Action or Decision: Whether or not to hit someone who hits me		
Choice(s)	**Positive Consequences**	**Negative Consequences**
Hit them.	It makes me feel good. He or she may not hit me next time because they know I'll hit back.	Trouble at school (insert punishment or consequence). Possible trouble at home?
Tell the teacher.	Don't get in trouble at school.	I'm a tattletale. Friends tease me, say I'm a wimp.
Do nothing.	Don't get in trouble at school.	I feel bad. They'll do it again because I didn't do anything.

The chart can work with other choices, and it's important to guide your students through the process often enough that they internalize it. Although this isn't a one-size-fits-all, quick-fix solution to any problem, it clearly shows that there are always choices. The enemy of an internal sense of control is the trapped feeling of a lack of choices. That simply isn't true 99% of the time. There may be only one good or acceptable choice, but there are always choices. And the moment we focus on that, we are much more likely to succeed and feel better about what we are doing.

This is simply an adaptation of the old strategy of making a list when you have a decision to make; list the positives and negatives about it. However, breaking out the specific choices is critical. For those of us with a strong sense of internal control, the choices are natural and embedded in our thought process. But students who feel helpless need to specify different options. And there is always a choice. For example, if I'm suspended from school, I can

- Groan, moan, and make a scene
- Get upset and act even worse when I come back
- Take my lumps, and deal with it—no matter what
- Play and enjoy the time off

If you work with young children, you may be thinking this is unsuitable. I disagree. When young children learn how to make good choices with basic things (sharing a toy, etc.), they make better decisions later. You can do this with young students (as young as kindergarten); just choose age-appropriate decisions, and use a happy face and sad face for the chart headings. Kids don't get in trouble because they take drugs—they are in trouble because they didn't make a decision early on to not be in that situation. So, although "just say no" is easy to say, it's even easier to avoid the situation altogether.

Making Dreams Real

You can encourage your students to have a dream through classroom activities. For example, you can have students write about their dreams: What do you want to be when you grow up? Kendra Alston has her students choose or write a theme song for their lives (see example). Many Olympic and professional athletes say they write their dreams on a card, and then look at it every morning to reinforce it. The day I wrote this chapter, I received an e-mail with this quote from California Governor Arnold Schwarzenegger: "I have my vision of what I want California to be and I don't care what it takes to make it reality. People used to ask me about how I could spend 5 hours a day lifting weights and doing the same sit ups over and over. It's simple. I see my vision very clearly and then I do whatever it takes to make it happen."

That's why it's important to write your dream; writing it down makes it real and helps you achieve it. Let your students be creative. The important thing is to give them the opportunity to dream and to express those dreams.

Theme Song

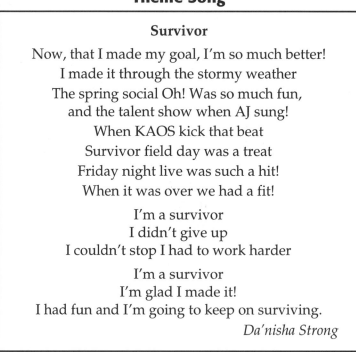

Survivor

Now, that I made my goal, I'm so much better!
I made it through the stormy weather
The spring social Oh! Was so much fun,
and the talent show when AJ sung!
When KAOS kick that beat
Survivor field day was a treat
Friday night live was such a hit!
When it was over we had a fit!

I'm a survivor
I didn't give up
I couldn't stop I had to work harder

I'm a survivor
I'm glad I made it!
I had fun and I'm going to keep on surviving.

Da'nisha Strong

Modeling

A third part of a dream-building classroom is to model having and achieving dreams. That starts with sharing your own dreams. If your dream is to write an article about your teaching, tell your students about it. If your dream is to travel to a new place, put a picture up near your desk so they (and you) will be reminded of it. Read stories about people and their dreams and goals for their lives. It's important to talk about people who achieved their dreams despite failures, such as those in the sample list of role models.

Role Models

Clay Aiken	Overcame issues with bullying during middle school to become runner-up on "American Idol"
Elizabeth Blackwell	America's first female physician, despite opposition from the medical community
Sally Ride	First American female astronaut
Grant Hill	Persevered to continue playing pro basketball after five traumatic left ankle injuries
Abraham Lincoln	Although from humble background and suffered several setbacks in his political career, became President of the United States
Wilma Rudolph	First American woman to win three gold medals after having been crippled by polio as a child
Laura-Beth Moore	At 12 years old, founded Houston's recycling program
Henry Winkler	Famous television actor overcame problems with dyslexia and dedicated his life to being a role model for kids

When possible, bring in speakers or resource materials that are linked to your students' dreams. For example, if you have a student who wants to be a painter, find a local artist to come into your classroom. If several of your students want to be pro basketball players and you don't have a pro star handy, bring in the star of the high school or college team. You'll be amazed at how much of a role model they can be for your students and how honored they are to be asked.

I've been in several school districts recently that have AVID (Advancement Via Individual Determination) classes. The program provides academic support in grades 5 to 12 for students who are typically performing at an average level but are capable of higher levels of performance. One of their goals is to "level the playing field for minority, rural, low-income, and other students without a college-going tradition in their families" (www.avidonline.org). Janet Gonski, AVID teacher at Crofton Middle School, described the goal as to "support them on the bottom so they can fly to the top." This is our goal for all of our students, to help them move beyond their limits.

Summary

- Establish a sense of self-empowerment in your students; it is essential to their success!
- Provide structures, activities, and modeling to facilitate positive beliefs in students.
- Help students recognize the choices they can make each and every day as well as their positive and negative consequences.
- Provide opportunities for students to verbalize their dreams and keep track of them in writing.
- Share your personal dreams with students along with stories of other people who have persevered to reach their dreams.

If you would like more information...

This site is about the AVID program: http://www.avidonline.org/.

The 7 Habits of Highly Effective Teens: The Ultimate Teenage Success Guide by Sean Covey, Simon & Schuster Adult Publishing Group.

The Eagles Who Though They Were Chickens by Mychal Wynn, Rising Sun Publishing.

Self-Efficacy: Raising the Bar for All Students, 2nd Edition by Joanne Eisenberger, Marcia Conti-D'Antonio, and Robert Bertrando, Eye On Education.

Staying With It: Role Models of Perseverance by Emerson Klees, Cameo Press.

O

Owners, Not Renters

The landscape should belong to the people who see it all the time.

LeRoi Jones (now known as Amiri Baraka)

Do you remember the first time you made a big purchase or invested in something really big that was yours? For me, it was my first car. I worked several summers as a lifeguard to save enough to buy a small red Toyota. It took all of my savings, but it was mine. I washed it, took care of it, and had a special pride in knowing that it was mine and that I had worked for it.

What about your students? How do they view the classroom? Is it yours, and they are simply renting space for a short time? Or do they feel like they own it with you, that it is *our* classroom? That may sound funny, but go back to your personal experience. How do you feel about things you own? My guess is you have extra stick-to-it-ness—a longer-term view about things you own. You are more invested in taking care of them and making them better.

I recently overheard a conversation between two neighbors at a garden shop. One was talking about planting bushes and flowers in the yard and the other said, "I don't do that, mine's just a rental." I am not disparaging everyone who rents, but when you own something you tend to have a different level of commitment. Now let us go back to your students. Is it *your* classroom or *our* classroom? The Y makes all the difference. Actually, the *why* makes all the difference. Too often, students feel like they are only in school because they are required to be there, and if they do not like what is happening, they can just wait it out and move on to the next place later. Compare that to students in classrooms where there is a sense of shared ownership. They love coming to school, and as one student told me, "It's my class, and if I'm not there, I'll be missed!"

You might be thinking, "I'll take the ones who want to be here, and for those other, well, after all, they are just here a year. If they want to have that attitude, it is okay with me; it is their choice. I can wait them out, too." A key part of motivation is feeling a sense of ownership in what is going on. Consider that students spend almost a third of every day in school; that is a lot of time. I talked to a parent who said, "We've just resigned ourselves to having a bad year. Michael just isn't 'into' school this year." We know that for many students, particularly those who are not performing on grade level, it takes them several years to make up for one bad year or for one year with a less effective teacher.

Think About It...

Think of a student you teach who doesn't feel any sense of ownership or belonging in your classroom or school. How does that student impact other students?

There is an individual impact on students who are not engaged in learning, but there is also an impact for the overall classroom community. It doesn't matter if you teach in a pre-K, elementary, middle, high school, college, or any other type of classroom. If you have even one student who doesn't feel like a part of the classroom (and that is really what ownership is about; feeling as though you belong), there is a ripple effect. Chances are, if Jan feels as though she is *just there*, she will act out and disrupt the learning of others. As a teacher it's important to have everyone working together. Remember the old saying, "In a TEAM, Together Everyone Achieves More"? In the most effective classrooms, all students believe they are valued, belong, and contribute to the overall well-being of the classroom.

There are two popular views of how classrooms should work. The first view is that schools should function like a factory with classrooms as an assembly line. Students line up, come in, learn, line up, go home, and repeat the sequence the next day. Most students do not thrive in that situation, and they rarely feel any sense of ownership.

Community of Learners

The second perspective views classrooms as a community of learners. The dictionary defines community in several ways, but I particularly like "ownership or participation in common." That would mean that a community of learners is a group with ownership or participation (in learning) in common. In this model most students thrive. Notice that this includes everyone who shares that learning; so it includes, but is not limited to, students. A true learning community includes everyone involved with that shared purpose, which includes students, teachers, parents, families, administrators, and anyone else related to the learning in your classroom.

Tracie Clinton at Cotton Belt Elementary School shares a perfect example of an activity that involves the entire learning community. She sponsors a *Fall for Reading* day in October. Her students come to school dressed in pajamas and slippers. Parents and local community members come in to read to the class, and they have fall treats such as apples and cider. She says, "The day is fun filled with reading, and needless to say, the kids enjoy themselves."

I was visiting a classroom where the teacher used a variety of symbolic elements in her classroom. Her class always had a name, t-shirts (she found a business partner to cover the costs), and a logo. The class even had a mission statement signed by all students, parents, and the principal to represent their commitment and support. However, the inclusion teacher was not asked to sign. One day, when she came in the room, a student said, "She's not really a part of us; if she was, her name would be on the poster." The teacher quickly remedied the situation and explained that, once again, she learned from her students. There are really two lessons in that example. First, be sure to include everyone; and second, symbolic elements help build and reinforce your community.

Think About It...

What symbols exist in your classroom? How would you change the symbols?

Ownership is a characteristic that takes time to encourage, but you can build it by focusing on three specifics: choice, voice, and leadership.

Choice

Offering choices is one of the simplest ways to encourage student involvement in your classroom. Unfortunately, I talk to many teachers and students who don't feel as though they have any choices at all. I talked to one student who told me he felt like school was a place where "they tell you what to do all the time." Feeling a lack of choice is disheartening and frustrating for anyone. There are many opportunities for students to have choices in your classroom.

One of the most basic ways is to allow students to choose how they demonstrate understanding of content. When I assigned a book report to my students, for example, they could choose the desired format. Some wrote a report, others made a poster or created a commercial. I've been in primary classrooms where students could choose whether to write, draw, or tell what they know about the lesson.

I was in an alternative school where students felt they had no choices. The English teacher was planning a unit on Shakespeare. As she and I talked, she realized that allowing her students to choose a final project would encourage stronger participation from them. However, she was uncomfortable simply letting them come up with whatever they wanted to do. She began by allowing them to explain the literary work by choosing from a list of appropriate projects, such as painting a mural, creating a music video, designing a commercial, or writing a children's book.

You could offer these options with just about any assignment you do, no matter the subject. Imagine the depth of understanding needed for a student to explain a concept in a two-minute commercial or the creativity involved in developing a music video to explain content. If they are allowed to choose how they show you they understand the content, many students will invest more time and effort on the task.

Voice

Student voice is actually taking the notion of choice to a higher level. With choices, you are still the primary decision maker; and you are allowing students to make some decisions, usually within some parameters. Voice is about students truly sharing in the decision-making process.

A simple way to do this is to adapt the K-W-L graphic organizer. In a K-W-L you ask the students what they already know about a topic (K) or what they think they know about it. Next, you ask what they want to know (W). Then, you teach the lesson, and ask them what they learned (L). With my students that encouraged passive learning. The message was subtle: We'll tell you, but you do all the teaching and we tell you what you taught.

I love a newer adaptation of this, which is a K-W-H-L. After students generate what they want to know, they also come up with how they could find out the answers to their questions (H). Think of how much that expands your instruction. Instead of you deciding the best way to learn everything, they help! If you are studying snakes, one of your students may have one at home. Another may have a parent who works at a zoo. Yet another student may have a book on snakes or a brother who wrote a report on snakes, which provides a great opportunity to talk about primary versus secondary source material. All of a sudden your students are involved in creating the instruction in your classroom.

K-W-H-L

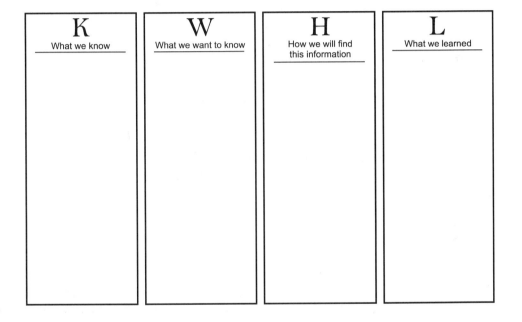

K What we know	W What we want to know	H How we will find this information	L What we learned

Adam Myers, a language arts teacher at Coulwood Middle School, used a controversial approach to spur his students to use their voices to express strong opinions. In the middle of a novel study, *Forged by Fire* by Sharon Draper (the story of a young boy's life as he attempts to protect his younger half-sister from mental, physical, and sexual abuse from their stepfather), Adam hid the books. When students asked for the books, he explained that parents were unhappy about the decision to read *Forged by Fire* and that the book was banned from the classroom because of the inappropriate subject matter in the book. The students quickly responded: "Whose parents told?" "The book isn't even that bad." "I hate this school!" "This is wrong." So he encouraged students to write letters to parents, the principal, the governor, or the president expressing how they felt about the book and what happened. All agreed that the novels belonged in their hands, no one had the right to take them away.

He then

> told them I was just kidding. I like to think of their laughter and comments about their mean teacher as relief that the books were still going to be a part of the classroom. What amazed me most...were the answers I received when I asked why I would do such a thing. It was in this conversation with my students that I saw that I had truly used literature and writing to help my students both academically and developmentally. They were attached to the characters and felt cheated that they wouldn't know the end of the plot. They took ownership of their writing as they justified that although the novel was controversial, it allowed them to explore a realistic situation that unfortunately was too close to some of their friends, classmates, or family members. My students have not forgiven me, and that is o.k. because I'm sure they will never forget me.

What a powerful lesson. He tapped into students' strong feelings of justice and choice with a real-life example of censorship to spark ownership of an issue. Although a controversial activity, it clearly had a lasting impact on his students.

Leadership

A final way to build ownership is to provide opportunities for each student to be a leader in your room. I think the best, most consistent examples of this happen in early childhood classrooms. There is a leader for the day listed on the board. Or there is a chart on the board and it lists the leaders for the day: the lunch line leader, the calendar leader, the recess leader, and so on. Every child has a specific role, and the teacher rotates those regularly. In that particular classroom, everyone is a leader at least once a week.

Allowing students the chance to be in charge is an important part of education. And for some of your students, your classroom is the only place they are given that opportunity. My first year of teaching, I had a young lady who was an absolute nightmare to have in class. She rebelled against everything, and I was convinced she would be my downfall. Finally, I asked her one day to be in charge of handing out papers. All of a sudden everything changed. She arrived to class early, handed out papers, and paid attention to everything I said. I overheard her tell another student that she was "Miss Blackburn's teaching assistant," so she had to behave in class. I was amazed, and realized how a simple request had completely changed her view of my class—she felt like it was hers, too, all because she had a leadership role.

Gin Sorrow shared a similar story with me: "I had some very social and unmotivated girls that were negative leaders in a class. I challenged them to teach the next section. They would come early in the mornings and work with me during planning times to prepare the lessons. It was a wonderful experience. I was able to see some of their methods for connecting with their peers that I could incorporate in to my teaching the rest of the year. The girls grew into more positive leaders and challenged the other students to improve. It is definitely a strategy I would use again."

Many teachers use more formal structures, such as electing class officers. There was a story in our local paper about a fifth grader who was constantly in and out of trouble. After three suspensions, his teacher decided to take a different approach. She held an election, he was voted class president, and his whole attitude changed.

Tamara Willis, seventh-grade social studies teacher at Sullivan Middle School chose a similar approach after her students complained, "School is like a job and…we should get paid for attending." They voted to create a business, which was named Sullivan University. Students prepared resumes and applied for positions (Dean, Professor, and Intern) and interviewed one another for the jobs. Those students who were hired to be deans held an executive board meeting with Ms. Willis to form teams and design new classroom rules to address issues related to poor behavior and absenteeism.

As the experiment continued, students began to demonstrate leadership by quieting their peers when they were disruptive. The result? Attendance increased, students were more engaged in instruction, and discipline referrals decreased. All these examples have one thing in common: The teachers chose to channel students' negative behaviors into positive action.

Ultimately, you have the final say in your classroom. After all, you are the teacher. But if you are willing to share that ownership with your students to create a true community of learners, you will also reap the benefits. Not only will your students want to come to class, so will you. In the opening quotation, LeRoi Jones (who is now known as Amiri Baraka) notes that the landscape should belong to those who see it the most. I believe that the classroom should belong, at least in part, to those who spend the most time there—the students.

Think About It...

What choices do your students have in your classroom? How are their voices heard? What are some examples of leadership roles students can take in your room?

Summary

- Create invested interest and ownership. Everyone is more passionate about an idea or concept in which they have invested interest. Likewise, the physical space in your classroom will be best used if your students feel some ownership in it.

- Create involvement as you build a community of learners. It is crucial for each and every student.

- Extend your learning community to parents, families, administrators, other school faculty and the community.

- Offer choices in assignments, assessments, and activities to encourage student involvement in your classroom.

- Allow students opportunities to share in the decision-making processes of your classroom. (This requires flexibility on your part!)

- Think of creative ways for each student to be a leader in your classroom.

- Allow the classroom to belong, at least in part, to those who spend the most time there—the students.

If you would like more information...

This site provides an article and resources about student-led conferences: http://www.educationworld.com/a_admin/admin/admin112.shtml/.

A Reason to Teach: Creating Classrooms of Dignity and Hope by James A. Beane, Heinemann.

Letting Children Take the Lead in Class, Education Journal by Ana Maria Andrade and Delia Hakim, ASCD.

"What Choice Do I Have?" Reading, Writing, and Speaking Activities to Empower Students by Terry Bigelow and Michael J. Vokoun, Heinemann.

P

Perception is Reality

Whether you think you can or whether you think you can't, you are probably right.

Henry Ford

A critical issue for students is their self-concept and perception of their own learning. I remember my first class of remedial readers. Some of them thought they already knew how to read well enough, so they didn't need to learn anything else. Others thought they didn't know anything; they couldn't learn; because if they could learn, they would have before now.

Both groups were wrong: Students in the first category still had more to learn, and my second group of students knew more than they realized and had potential to learn more. However, in both cases, their perceptions outweighed the realities of the situation. In fact, their perceptions were all that mattered to them. You probably have students in both of these groups—the ones who have given up on themselves and the ones who are convinced they know enough even when they don't.

I am reminded of a story my dad told me about the purpose of education. He explained that his favorite definition was based on the work of John Dewey as interpreted by a third-grade teacher. The teacher said the purpose of learning is to "figure out what to do when you don't know what to do." This exemplifies the difference between those who are motivated, strategic learners, and those who aren't. The first student knows how to do this, the

109

second one doesn't. But there are many beliefs and actions embedded in this difference that stand in direct contrast to each other.

Shane

Shane is a student with lots of potential. His fourth-grade teacher sees this and has identified several particularly strong talents. He is creative, which comes out in his writing on the rare occasions when he writes without worrying about what he is writing. However, he doesn't trust his own judgment or opinion. In the initial stages of an assignment, he will pepper the teacher with questions—asking over and over again what he is supposed to do and bringing even initial, vague ideas to the teacher to see if he is "doing it right." When he writes, his favorite time is the peer review; but instead of taking specific suggestions and implementing them, he continues to ask everyone for their opinions: "Here's what I'm thinking...here's what she said. What do you think? What do you think? What do you think?" ad nauseam. One person's opinion isn't enough, even if it's his teacher's or parent's opinion. Something is only "true" if everyone says so, and of course, that rarely happens.

In social settings, Shane succumbs to peer pressure; he goes along with the crowd, whether he agrees with what they are doing or not. Shane actually is friends with Rick, the newest student at school; but when several other boys decided to tease Rick on the playground, Shane joined in.

Do you have a Shane in your classroom? The underlying issue here is an external frame of reference—there is no internal belief or confidence in his ability or judgment. He places a high value on the opinions of others, which means he seeks constant reassurance and asks for help before trying to work out any problems on his own. He also regularly submits to peer pressure.

José

Contrast Shane with José. José is also a creative student, who loves to write and illustrate long stories. He gets completely immersed in his work and can be found drafting more ideas any time he has an extra minute. He will do peer review sessions because the teacher requires them; he listens to feedback, but he goes ahead with what he thinks is best with his writing. He prefers individual writing conferences with the teacher but wants to wait until he has worked through his own issues with his writing first. He asks his teacher about specific issues he is struggling with, rather than just asking "What do you think?" At times, he may even disagree with his teacher. If so, he explains his view and negotiates with the teacher for a better option. When he's in the lunchroom and a group of students want him to participate in teasing or other questionable behavior, José politely refuses and goes his own way.

José has a strong internal locus of control. He is confident in his own decisions, he prefers to ask for help only when his own toolkit of strategies doesn't work, and he consistently stands up to his peers when he believes they are wrong.

You probably have both of these students in class and some students who incorporate characteristics of each. What can you do as a teacher to help the Shanes in your class? Steve Siebold, a former junior tennis pro and Mental Toughness consultant, compares the thought processes of the amateur performer and the professional performer. They are remarkably applicable to students such as Shane and José. After all, what we ask students to do in learning is performance to them! We can adapt Steve's comparative categories to learning: As depicted in the example (see the next page), Amateurs are nonstrategic learners; professionals are strategic learners.

Let's look at some of these beliefs and how they impact the issue of motivation.

Trusting Yourself

When working with students like Shane, begin by recognizing the real issue. He isn't simply bugging you, he truly doesn't trust or believe in himself or his judgment. There is no short-term solution to changing beliefs, but there are actions you can take to support students like Shane. First, when he comes to you for help, don't just give him the answer, which may only encourage the dependency. Instead, ask him what he thinks and keep asking until you get an answer. You may have to encourage, wait, or ask multiple times; but keep at it until Shane starts thinking about what he's asking. Provide positive reinforcement when he attempts to figure it out independently first, even if he isn't right. Then provide more positive reinforcement for ultimately solving the problem himself.

Amateur Versus Pro

Nonstrategic (Amateur) Learners	Strategic (Professional) Learners
Overwhelmed by problems	Deals with one problem at a time
Places high value on the opinions of others (needs constant reassurance)	Is confident of own decisions
Regularly submits to peer pressure	Stands up to peers
External frame of reference	Internal locus of control
Views failure as the end, not as a learning process	Learns from failures; views failure as a learning process
Expects to do the same things and get different results	Realizes that you must change what you do to get different results
Asks for help first without trying to work out problem on own	Asks for help only after using toolkit of own strategies
Doesn't think about thinking (no metacognition)	Thinks about thinking a lot, even without realizing it (metacognition)
No plans for what to do if instructions don't work	Plans for the unexpected and deals with those things; has alternate plans
Doesn't connect learning to other things unless made explicit by the teacher; doesn't realize that all connects to long term	Thinks about the "what if..." always making connections in head to self, other learning experiences, and future and real life
Cannot visualize an end product or a correct result of task or learning; doesn't know what it "feels like to be right"	Can visualize the end product or result of task or learning; is confident of correctness and/or being right
Uses feedback and criticism as a stop sign	Uses feedback and criticism to improve

You might also allow him to ask some other students for help, but that should be limited. I have been in many classrooms where teachers have a rule that students have to "Ask three before me," meaning they have to ask three students before they ask the teacher a question. It's like any other routine, if you take time to teach it to students, you gain more time later. Just think of how many times students come to you for basic, simple questions: What page did you say? Which problems? Where did you say to put this paper?

Viewing Failure

A second difference between the strategic and nonstrategic learner is how students view failure. Some students expect to be perfect on the first try. Don't we all want that? But when it doesn't happen, there are two choices. For struggling, unmotivated students, anything short of being right (which includes receiving feedback and/or constructive criticism) becomes a stop sign—a symbol of failure. The voice in Shane's head says, "Because you missed it on the first try, you're a failure, so you might as well give up." This is compounded by the fact that Shane had no plan for what to do if what he was told to do did not work. He copied the example off the board, he tried the practice problem that way, and it didn't work. Therefore, he considered himself a failure. It didn't cross his mind that you showed one example and that, depending on the question, he might have to adapt what you showed him to do.

In this situation, you'll need to be clear, model adaptations, and provide extra scaffolding and support. A related issue is that nonstrategic learners expect to do the same thing and get different results. So, the last time he had to do a project, Shane waited until the last minute, didn't have the resources to complete it, and made an F. For the next project, he did the same thing; he didn't see that working ahead of time and pulling together resources in advance will make the difference.

This contrasts with strategic learners, who use feedback and criticism to improve because they view failure as a learning process. They recognize that failure happens to everyone, and that success comes from building off failures. Strategic learners make plans for the unexpected. Playing "what if" allows them to deal with the unexpected. They also recognize that you must change what you do to get different results, which comes from a strong internal belief that they are responsible for results.

With my students, I openly discussed the role of failure in success; giving personal examples as appropriate to show that everybody fails. By the way, I still do this with my graduate students, who sometimes view me as someone who never fails. We all have times when we are not successful; it's important to show students how to overcome those times. Find reading selections about people who have overcome failure to achieve and build lessons about these role models into your regular instruction. Also, encourage your students who do try, particularly if they are unsuccessful on the first attempt.

Thinking About Thinking

Strategic learners actively think about their thinking; they monitor their thinking. These students are *active thinkers*. During instruction, they are always making connections in their head. They connect what you are teaching to their own experiences, other things they have learned, and how this would apply to their life. Think of their brains as a connect-the-dots puzzle. They are always looking to slot that information into the puzzle and connect it to other points.

On the other hand, nonstrategic learners don't even realize they are thinking, even when they are thinking negative thoughts. They don't automatically connect learning to themselves or any other content unless it is made explicit by the teacher. They don't see any relationship between their lives and what you are teaching. What is the puzzle in their head? A word search puzzle, with information hidden inside other letters, and they don't know where to look.

What can a teacher do to help students who struggle with connections? First, a teacher can scaffold the connections process. Instead of simply pointing out the connections for students, guide them to the connections through questioning and graphic organizers. One of my favorites is the text relationship guide (see Text Connection Guide on page 115). Second, you can share your own thinking processes to provide a model for your students.

Text Connection Guide

How (insert name of text) relates to:	
Something else I've read…	Something I've learned in another class…
Something in my life…	

Dealing with Problems

Another issue relates to how students deal with problems. Nonstrategic learners are overwhelmed by problems; and because most new experiences are seen as problems, this happens a lot. Strategic learners may have many problems to deal with, but they simply start dealing with them, one at a time. Have you ever talked to one of your students who said, "I don't know where to start"? That's the nonstrategic learner: so snowed under by the sheer weight of the task, it's safer to do nothing. As a teacher, that's why it is so critical to chunk assignments or tasks. Putting a list of the steps for completion on the board and then guiding students to creating their own lists over time is helpful to prevent overwhelming the nonstrategic learner. Adding time elements to the chunks can also assist. I frequently break down tasks into manageable bites and give students five minutes for this one, or two minutes or ten minutes—whatever you think is reasonable. You can adjust as you go. This also helps nonstrategic learners stay focused on the immediate task at hand.

Visualizing Success

Finally, nonstrategic learners are less likely to visualize an end product or a correct result of a task; they simply don't know what it "feels like to be right." Much of the lack of self-confidence stems from this: They have no internal feeling of success on which to build. In this case it is particularly important to show models of student work at varying levels and talk through the *why* of the grade or level of success. Also, you need to remind students of times they have been right, perhaps even have them keep a running list of successes so they can refer to it. If you think about it, some of your students really don't have a frame of reference of any school successes they have. Start today by helping them build such a frame. It's like building a house; one brick or success at a time.

Summary

- Make your goal to have students become strategic learners who see failures as part of the learning process, not stop signs.
- Recognize the real issues behind a student's actions.
- Continuously encourage students to become more responsible and independent learners.
- Build up a students' toolboxes of strategies to use when they encounter problems they need to solve independently.
- Provide opportunities for success and sincere praise to build a student's internal confidence.
- Openly discuss the role of failure in success by giving personal examples and sharing stories of historical figures who have overcome obstacles.
- Teach students to be active thinkers by helping them interact with texts and make connections with what they are learning.
- Break down seemingly enormous goals into smaller, more manageable chunks, if necessary, for a student to perceive it as attainable.
- Allow students to taste success at least once; they are more likely to strive for success again.

If you would like more information...

101 Secrets of the World Class by Steve Siebold, London House.

Staying With It: Role Models of Perseverance by Emerson Klees, Cameo Press.

Unstoppable: 45 Powerful Stories of Perseverance and Triumph from People Just Like You by Cynthia Kersey, SourceBooks, Inc.

Q

Quantify Quality

Alice is lost and asks the Cheshire Cat, "Which way should I go from here?" The Cat responds, "Where do you want to end up?" Alice says she doesn't care, then the cat says, "Then it really doesn't matter which way you walk."

From *Alice in Wonderland* by Lewis Carroll

A particular issue for many students is not knowing what good looks like. We ask students to complete an assignment, and we are frustrated when the quality of work does not match our expectations. This leads us to question whether or not the student cares about doing the work or wonder if the student tried at all. But, many of our most frustrated—and frustrating—students simply don't know what to do, how to do it, or they think what they are doing is right.

This often occurs when you ask students to answer questions that require more than just reciting facts, such as describing the causes of an event in history, persuading the reader of a position, or explaining how to solve a math problem. Each type of question requires higher-level thinking skills and applying all those facts they memorized. Chances are, your at-risk students don't do well with these types of questions or similar assignments such as reports or projects. Again, don't assume that it's because they don't want to or just aren't doing it. Many students simply don't know how to do this correctly. As teachers, it is our job to activate or provide background knowledge with content, as well as process. In this chapter, we'll look at a framework for making performance expectations explicit.

First, start by discussing the assignment with students: "One task you'll need to complete to be successful in my class is to answer essay questions appropriately. How many of you have written answers to essay questions before?" Students respond. "What did you have to do to make a good grade on them?" Again, students respond. Typical answers include: "Must be at least three paragraphs." "Must be at least five sentences." "Everything must be spelled correctly." Write these on the board or an overhead transparency (remember, visual reinforcement is important). Discuss the answers, clarifying misconceptions. Most of the time, you don't grade based on the number of sentences; that may reflect depth, but many times it doesn't.

Second, show a sample of a *good or acceptable* answer to a question. Be sure to tell students this is an example you would consider to be good. Have students read the sample or read it with them. Discuss what you are looking for in an answer. It's important that your expectations are clear. Before this class decide on your key criteria for what makes a good answer, and state those in terms that are understandable to students.

In my experience, teachers generally expect the following:

- Answer the question. Be on point and don't include irrelevant information.

- Provide supporting details and examples for your statements.
  I told my students that writing is like a chair: The seat is your statement, and each supporting detail is a leg of the chair. If you only have one leg of the chair, it isn't stable—just like your writing. If you only write one example, the writing isn't as strong. Again, visuals help students see what you are talking about. Remember, we live in an MTV world.

- Have a good introduction and conclusion; start and finish well.

- Don't make so many writing mistakes with grammar and spelling that I can't read your paper.
  You typically want minimal or no errors, but you don't want students to focus on this first.

Discuss what you are looking for: "Just as there are discipline rules in a school to ensure order and acceptable behavior, there are basic procedures to follow to be successful with learning. First, you need to answer the question. Sometimes students will put in extra information that doesn't answer the question, because they think they need more words or sentences. That can actually make your answer worse." Continue to describe other rules. "Just as a reminder, for the first few weeks of school, I will post the procedures." Show the poster on your wall that lists the criteria and provides visual reinforcement.

Third, gently discuss the differences between your procedures and their experiences. Don't tell your students they are wrong; explain that you want them to understand what they need to do to be successful in your class: "You'll notice that my rules are a little different from what you told me you did last year. Although you can't really answer my questions with just a sentence or two, I don't just count the number of words or sentences. I look at whether you actually answered the question, whether or not you gave at least three examples to support your answer, and so on. I know this may be a little different, so let's see what that actually looks like." Show a sample answer on the board, the overhead, or in a handout; and point out exactly how the sample meets your expectations. Be sure to give specific examples.

Fourth, give students another sample answer, preferably on a handout. Pair students and have them read the answer and decide whether or not it follows the rules. You might even have them guess the grade, but I usually start just with satisfactory or not satisfactory rather than A, B, or C. Lead a whole-class discussion, going to each of your rules and asking students whether or not the sample meets the rule and why or why not: "Let's talk about how this answer matches the criteria. The first guideline is that a question should answer the question. The question was [insert sample here]. Does this answer actually answer that?" Students respond. "Can you tell me where exactly in the essay it answers the question?" Again, allow students to respond.

Fifth, using the same process, provide a second example to give students another chance to practice looking for good responses. As they write their own answers, explain that they need to do the same things. If students are hung up on particular misconceptions such as always needing three paragraphs, give them a model that does so but is bad in other ways so they can see the difference in criteria.

Sixth, give them a question to answer, reminding them that they should complete the answer using your rules. Pick a simple question; your focus in this lesson is on the process of writing a good answer rather than demonstrating they understand new content. That is ultimately your desired result, but let's do the basics first. Remember, if students don't know where they want to go (a good response), they also don't know how to walk (how to get there).

Finally, have them either write down the guidelines from your poster or give them a writer's checklist to use as they complete their short essay. During the next lesson or the next day, review the rules with your students through an interactive discussion. As you go through each rule, ask them to look at their own essays to check if they followed the rule. Have them physically check each rule on the paper or the checklist. Then pair them up again to check each other's papers, again rule by rule, while you move around the room monitoring their work. Give them the chance to rewrite their answers before they turn them in for a grade.

Working through this process with your students takes several days and may need to be revisited throughout the year. Also, the use of rubrics supports this process. Providing students with a clear set of clarifying statements for each criteria on your procedures chart can help them improve their writing throughout the year.

Strategy In Action

Let me share an example of how one school implemented this strategy to quantify quality. Sixth-grade teachers at Chestnut Oaks Middle School in Sumter, South Carolina, met at the beginning of the school year and agreed on a common set of guidelines for writing answers to essay questions or short essays in all content areas. In our workshop they came up with several criteria they expect but struggled with making these guidelines too specific and simple enough for students to understand. One teacher described the comparison of a good conclusion being like a good landing on a plane (not too bumpy), so we worked together to develop all the rules around the concept of a plane. This concept fit with their overall grade-level *Soaring to Success* theme and is easily understandable by students. (See Taking Off with Writing.)

To provide a common experience for students as they adjust to middle school, the teachers reinforce these expectations throughout the curriculum. The language arts teachers introduced the concept described in this chapter. However, the next week social studies teachers reviewed the rules and showed samples that are oriented toward social studies. Then, their students practiced answering a social studies question. In week three science teachers followed with specific examples and practice; and in the fourth week of the process, math teachers showed students how the same process applies to writing an explanation of the solution of a problem. By week five of school, their students had a solid foundation for the school year and understood that there are key principles for success across all content areas.

Taking Off with Writing

Luggage

Supplies
Brain

Preparation for takeoff

Brainstorming method
Pilot's checklist

Smooth takeoff (beginning)

Restate the question
Well developed introduction

Flight (middle)

Smooth flight

Smooth landing

Well developed conclusion

Final check

Complete pilot's checklist

You may be thinking this isn't practical for you; it sounds like a tremendous amount of work to teach something your students should be able to do before they come to your class. I know I thought my students should be able to explain an answer in a paragraph by the seventh grade. Our choice is to complain or help our students learn. The time investment pays off with an overall increased quality of responses. Ideally, you should do this at the beginning of the school year; but if you are in the middle of the school year, don't put off trying this strategy for another year. Better late than never. It really is simple: Define what you are looking for (where you want to go), explain it to your students, and show them examples (the road to take). Too often, we are so busy covering the content, we forget to do the basics of the process.

Many students need to understand what is in your head. One teacher told me, "Most students turn in their best idea of what we are looking for. Sometimes they really don't know what we are thinking, and it's our job to make sure they do know." I think that defines this strategy more than anything else: Motivate your students by making sure they actually understand what they are expected to do.

Summary

- It's your job to make sure students know exactly what you are looking for.
- You should begin new assignments by discussing or surveying students' prior knowledge on the given topic.
- Students need to see what *good* or *acceptable* looks like in your eyes.
- Your expectations should be clear; communicate key criteria for what makes a good answer.
- You may have your students evaluate a sample answer to assess their understanding of the criteria you are looking for.
- Your students are more likely to be motivated to complete an assignment if they think they can do it successfully.

If you would like more information...

This site contains information on looking at student work: http://www.lasw.org/.

This site contains information on how to show students what good study skills look like: http://www.resourceroom.net/older/ida_studyskills.asp/.

A Facilitator's Book of Questions: Resources for Looking Together at Student and Teacher Work by David Allen and Tina Blythe, Teachers College Press.

This site contains Chestnut Oaks Middle School's rules for writing at grades six, seven, and eight: http://coms.sumter17.k12.sc.us.

R

Rigor is *Not* a Four-Letter Word

Smooth seas do not make skillful sailors.

African Proverb

Think About It...

Think about the last test you gave or the lesson you taught yesterday. What percentage of the questions asked had one right answer? What percentage had more than one possible answer?

What is rigor? Just saying the word aloud sounds harsh, doesn't it? In the dictionary rigor is defined as "the action of taking great care and being thorough in making sure something is correct." But what does rigor really mean in the classroom? And why do we assume students don't like rigorous work? In education today rigor is like silly putty; everyone wants to play with it (just do a Google search and see what you find with the term *academic rigor*); but once you get it, it's messy and seems to slip out of your hands.

What Exactly Is Rigor and Why Should I Care?

One of my favorite books on this topic is *Teaching What Matters Most*. Strong, Silver, and Perrini (2001) provide one of the best explanations of rigor and multiple tips and classroom examples. They define rigor as "the goal of helping students develop the capacity to understand content that is complex, ambiguous, provocative, and personally or emotionally challenging" (p. 7). As you think about that definition, you realize that rigor is not just about difficulty. In fact, the authors point out that it is important because it teaches students to use their full attention on a task; it helps students learn to deal with uncertainty; it helps develop perseverance; and it builds self-confidence.

But My Students…

There are two common misconceptions that are stumbling blocks on the road to rigor. First, we say that some students can't do harder work, which relates back to our expectation level of their abilities. I can assure you of one thing: If you don't believe your students can do something, they will go out of their way to prove you right.

Next, we assume that students do not like hard work. Of course students tell you they don't want to do something that requires more work. (Didn't you say the same thing when you were in school?) This is partly just their defenses going up: "Wait a minute! Harder? More challenging? What if I can't?" And if you teach older students, they'll say one thing to you when their friends are around; but they'll have a completely different answer if no one else is listening.

I facilitate Making Middle Grades Work assistance teams for the Southern Regional Education Board (SREB). Schools invite a team to come to their middle school to provide feedback for school improvement. My favorite parts of the visit is interviewing students. You discover so much more information from them that you simply wouldn't get otherwise. One of the questions is: "Quality learning is the result of considerable effort to do something exceedingly well. Give an example of an experience that required you to work hard and in which you did well." The answer I have heard most often is a special project, such as something they did for the science fair. Just about every time, they struggle to even think of an answer.

Students actually associate feelings of success and satisfaction with challenging work when it is accompanied by appropriate support. They also believe that hard work is important. Kids are insightful; if you give them busy work, they immediately recognize it for what it is. But if you engage them in authentic, real-life problem solving at high levels of challenge, they know you value and respect them.

Ratcheting Up the Level of Rigor in Your Classroom

I overheard a parent say, "The only way to increase rigor in my child's school is to change the curriculum." That's not true. You can increase rigor by changing how you teach your curriculum standards. But remember that increasing what you expect from your students must be accompanied by appropriate support and clear guidelines for grading.

Increase Complexity of Questions or Assignments

Chapter U, Understanding More than the Basics, is full of information on levels of questioning, so in this chapter I'm going to focus on increasing the complexity of assignments or projects. Too often, we ask students to solve a problem they just don't care about. I still remember one from my high school Algebra One class: A train leaves New York going 50 mph. Another train leaves Los Angeles going 65 mph. Then there was something about distance and median rates. Who cares? I didn't then, and I'm not sure I do now.

I was in a math classroom recently where students loved to solve word problems. The teachers developed a unit on roller coasters, so the students were discussing slope, distance, speed, and a variety of other math concepts so they could design the *perfect* roller coaster. It was a rigorous assignment. The complexity and ambiguity challenged students, and the students felt a connection because of their personal interest in the problem. You can give students a set of 50 problems for them to practice computational skills, or you can provide those opportunities for them to work together to truly apply those skills.

Raise Level of Difficulty of the Content

Another way to increase rigor is to boost the difficulty level of the content. On one of my school evaluation visits, a young girl stopped me in the hall. She asked why I was in the school; and when I explained, she asked if I would tell her teachers something without using her name. I agreed, and she said, "Do you think you could tell them that they teach a lot of things we already know? I mean, we did most of this when we were in elementary school." I am not suggesting that you stop reviewing content that your students don't understand. What I am saying is that if a student doesn't understand that a noun is a person, place, or thing by the time they are in the eighth grade, they aren't going to understand it when you explain it again.

I struggled with that, too. I had students who simply did not understand basic concepts, so I tried to teach them again; and it didn't work. What did work was following rigor rule number one: increasing the complexity of the assignment by moving to a more difficult, authentic purpose for using that knowledge, and then answering their questions to help them complete the assignment. Sometimes the more rigorous, authentic activity is easier for students simply because it makes sense to them.

For example, I told my students they had to create a classified ad to sell a product of their choice. I gave them envelopes with free words, but if they needed different words, they had to pay for them. The word cards contained adjectives, adverbs, and everything except nouns. One group tried to write the ad only using free words and quickly discovered that didn't work. At some point you have to tell someone what you are selling! It was a great lesson on the purpose of nouns and was much more effective than the standard review.

One major opportunity area for increasing the difficulty level of content is through the text materials used during teaching. Many times teachers use reading material that is too easy for students. I was in one an elementary school classroom where the students loved to read. But, as I talked with the students, I learned that part of the reason they loved to read was because it was so easy. Keyshawn told me, "I never have to read anything hard. If I get to a word I don't know, my teacher lets me pick another book." It's important for students to read a book or an article they can quickly and easily read; those opportunities build self-confidence, provide enjoyable experiences, and may increase student motivation.

But if students only read easy content, they never learn how to deal with more challenging materials. It's important for students to read something where there are new words, so they have to use the strategies they've learned to figure out the text on their own. I was explaining this in a workshop, and a teacher said, "That's not how we do it. I think students should experience challenging texts but only with teacher guidance. We do have students read at their instructional level [her term for more challenging material], but never on their own. When they are practicing independently, it should be easy."

I respectfully disagree. Don't give students something to read on their own that is completely above their heads, but you should give them appropriate opportunities to independently read challenging material after providing advance instruction and support. This approach assumes your goal is to develop independent learners who can capably handle our complex and changing world.

One tool I would recommend for selecting text materials is the Lexile Framework, which is a tool for looking at a reader's ability in relation to the difficulty of text. A readability formula, it allows you to understand a reader's performance (whether on a standardized test or informal assessment) through examples of text materials (books, newspapers, or magazines) the reader can understand. It is linked to many standardized tests, including the Stanford 9, the Terra Nova, and the Iowa Test of Basic Skills. The Lexile Framework provides a way to level books along a *reading thermometer* in a way that is truly proportional to the standardized test used (see the example). When I was teaching, I used books that were labeled on grade level, but in reality they were much easier than what students were expected to read on the state test. That is still true today, which is why it is important to use a measure that is consistent across all texts, including standardized tests.

Lexiles in Action

Ramón loves to read books by Gary Paulsen; however, he is comfortable with the Dunc and Amos series, which are in the 500 Lexile range. What Ms. Sheets knows about Ramón (from his testing information and her own observations) is that his actual Lexile level is 750. Using her knowledge of Lexiles, Ms. Sheets can suggest other Gary Paulsen books for Ramón to read.

Title	Lexile
Legend of Red Horse Cavern	470
Captive	600
Grizzly	720
Dogsong	930
Hatchet	1020
Brian's Winter	1140

Lexile

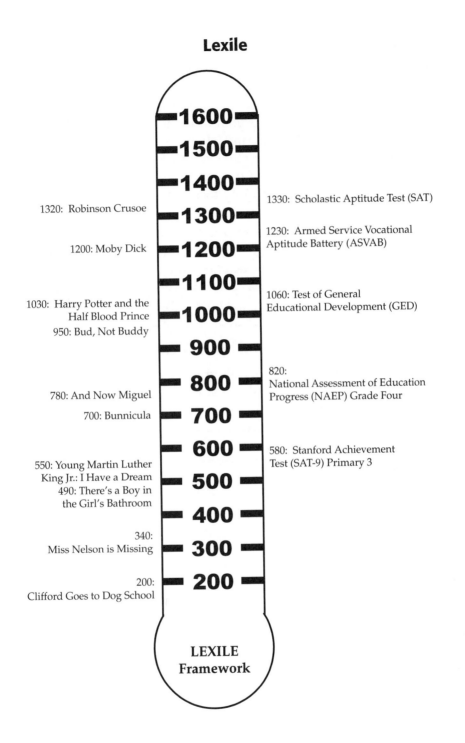

1320: Robinson Crusoe

1330: Scholastic Aptitude Test (SAT)

1230: Armed Service Vocational
Aptitude Battery (ASVAB)

1200: Moby Dick

1030: Harry Potter and the
Half Blood Prince

1060: Test of General
Educational Development (GED)

950: Bud, Not Buddy

820:
National Assessment of Education
Progress (NAEP) Grade Four

780: And Now Miguel

700: Bunnicula

580: Stanford Achievement
Test (SAT-9) Primary 3

550: Young Martin Luther
King Jr.: I Have a Dream
490: There's a Boy in
the Girl's Bathroom

340:
Miss Nelson is Missing

200:
Clifford Goes to Dog School

1600
1500
1400
1300
1200
1100
1000
900
800
700
600
500
400
300
200

LEXILE
Framework

Increase Expectations for Success

A final way to increase rigor is to increase your criteria for success. I've talked to many teachers who say, "As long as I get anything from my students, I'm happy." That attitude undercuts any attempts to increase rigor in your classroom. Part of respecting your students is expecting high-quality work from each one, while considering where a student truly is on the learning continuum. I am not advocating that you expect special needs student to give you 20-page research papers if they aren't able to do that. I am suggesting that you give them the opportunity to attempt to do more than minimal levels of work.

The first thing this requires is that you define high quality. We briefly discussed rubrics in Chapter K, Keys to Evaluation, and those are an effective way for you to determine your expectations for quality. However, I've seen rubrics in which the level of *best* was pretty mediocre. And if you don't have anything for comparison, you may unknowingly lower your standards.

Think About It...

Assume you want a group of eighth-grade students to read an article and make inferences and predictions. How would you define *needs work, good,* and *advanced*?

SREB offers detailed descriptions of proficiency levels tied to the National Assessment of Educational Progress (NAEP) test levels for middle school students. For the goal of making inferences and predictions, here's how they define the benchmarks for eighth graders:

Basic	Proficient	Advanced
<ul><li>Identify an author's stated position.</li><li>Make simple inferences about events and actions that have already occurred, characters' backgrounds, and setting.</li><li>Predict the next action in a sequence.</li></ul>	<ul><li>Use evidence from text to infer an author's unstated position.</li><li>Identify cause and effect in fiction and nonfiction.</li><li>Predict a character's behavior in a new situation using details from the text.</li><li>Formulate an appropriate question about causes or effects of actions.</li></ul>	<ul><li>With evidence from a nonfiction piece, predict an author's viewpoint on a related topic.</li><li>Describe the influence of an author's background on his or her work.</li><li>Recognize allusions.</li></ul>

How did your answers compare? One of the findings from research conducted by SREB is that many teachers expect advanced students to perform at the proficient level, and on grade–level students to perform at a basic level of competency. I've shared these and other competency indicators at many exit conferences after a visit. Teachers typically respond that they didn't realize they weren't expecting high levels of challenge.

It's important to compare our expectations with other published standard expectation levels. But it's also important to simply sit down with other teachers and discuss what your expectations should be. I recommend that you first talk with others who teach your same subject and grade level. Then meet with teachers one grade level above yours. Ask questions such as, "What do you expect students to know before they come into your class? From your perspective, what are the overall strengths students bring into your classroom? What are some areas that students across the board struggle with?" Finally, meet with teachers one grade level below yours. You'll discover new information that will help guide your instruction for the coming year.

Where Do I Start?

You may have read a newspaper article comparing students in the United States to those in other countries. That data likely came from the Third International Math and Science Study (TIMSS). The report compared instructional practices in the different countries, and one in particular is applicable here. In Japan, "Teachers begin by presenting students with a mathematics problem employing principles they have not yet learned. They then work alone or in small groups to devise a solution. After a few minutes, students are called on to present their answers; the whole class works through the problems and solutions, uncovering the related mathematical concepts and reasoning" (http://www.naplesnews.com/npdn/pe_columnists/article/0,2071,NPDN_14960_3096935,00.html; last accessed August 15, 2005).

In the United States we often do the opposite. We start with formulas and have students apply it in a real-life problem. That is a key difference. Do you believe that real-life problem solving is the *beginning* or the *end*? We do students a disservice when we don't provide challenging work. We live in a world that requires us to deal with complex, ambiguous, and sometimes frustrating problems. Only by presenting our students with opportunities to learn how to handle rigorous work in an instructional setting will they be prepared for life.

Summary

- Arouse curiosity with a rigorous curriculum and its intricate design, personal or emotional challenge, and openness to individual interpretation.

- Remember that students appreciate and respect authentic, challenging assignments.

- Require students to understand your content at a higher level by providing activities that ask them to use analytical and evaluative thinking.

- Be creative in your approach. Students need a variety of challenging activities that allow them to think outside the box.

- Provide frequent opportunities for students to engage in difficult (yet reasonable) texts.

- Reconsider your idea of high quality. Are your expectations set at a level where your students must strive to succeed?

- Present your students with the opportunities to learn how to handle rigorous work in an instructional setting so they will be prepared for life.

If you would like more information...

This site contains a rigor and relevance framework for classroom teachers: http://www.leadered.com/rigor.html/.

This site contains informatin about The *Lexile Framework*: http://www.lexile.com/.

Getting Students Ready for High School Series (set): http://www.sreb.org/main/publications/catalog/CatalogDisplaySub.asp?SubSectionID=42 SREB/.

Teaching What Matters Most by Richard Strong, Harvey Silver, and Matthew Perini, ASCD.

$\int$

Scaffolding for Success

With a definite, step-by-step plan—ah, what a difference it makes! You cannot fail, because each step carries you along to the next, like a track...

Scott Reed

Think About It...

What is the hardest thing you have ever learned to do? What do you remember about the learning process?

When I think about all the things I've learned, I can categorize them into the things I had to learn (for whatever reason—school or job—I was told to learn them) and things I learned because I wanted to, such as learning to swim, paint, and cook. And when I just think about those I chose to learn, there are some common characteristics about my learning process. First, I was excited to get started but typically found that whatever I was learning was harder or more complicated than I thought it would be. Next, if it got too hard and I couldn't find the right help, I would quit. And if that happened, it left a bad taste in my brain about ever doing it again.

Several years ago, I went on vacation with my parents and my sister Becky. One day, because of inclement weather, we stayed in the condo. They wanted to play canasta, and because you need four people to play, they needed me to join in. I didn't know how, so they offered to teach me. I was miserable. I didn't really want to play but gave in to family pressure. That was the first strike: learning something I didn't want to. Next, I knew nothing about the game, and it didn't seem to relate to any other game I did know. That was strike two: a lack of connection to any of my prior knowledge.

Now, my dad was my partner and an excellent coach, but this was a nightmare. They taught me basic rules and we played a practice game, which I suppose was a version of guided practice. Dad would tell me tips while we played, particularly reinforcing if I made a good play (positive reinforcement was the one good thing in the situation). However, once I got the basics down, we started playing for real; and that's where the trouble started. With every play it seemed like there was a new rule they had not told me, I could barely remember the basic rules, and we were playing at an advanced level. And of course I am competitive and really enjoy winning, so I was frustrated that we were losing. I suffered through several rounds and finally just quit.

Now, think of how often students in classrooms experience the same frustrations during the learning process. They come into class, are told to learn something, don't understand what it is or how it relates to anything else they know or are interested in, try it, and feel like the rules change as they go along. I heard a fourth grader explain it this way: "I thought I knew what she said, but I guess she said it different from what I heard." This isn't to recommend against teaching students to apply knowledge in other settings; but as students grow in their learning, they need support through the transitions.

Riding a Bike

A good comparison for this approach is learning to ride a bike. I remember riding a tricycle when I was growing up. I was good at it and felt confident of my abilities. At some point I got a *real bike* for Christmas. My parents wisely put training wheels on it while I learned to ride. Those extra wheels provided stability and balance as I learned how to ride it. Then Dad took the training wheels off. He taught me to ride without the training wheels, but he was beside me with one hand on the seat. One day he let go of the seat, and I realized I was riding by myself. I was so excited. I had learned to ride a bike and I loved it. I had confidence in my abilities, which enhanced my enjoyment.

According to the dictionary, a scaffold is "a temporary wooden or metal framework for supporting workmen and materials during the erecting, repairing, or painting of a building, etc." To adapt that for learning, scaffolding is a temporary verbal, visual, or physical framework for supporting students and resources during the formation, development, and enhancement of learning. It's really just a technical word for helping students learn, and I'm guessing you do it sometimes without realizing it. It's important to remember to provide scaffolding, which can be help by giving information, reminders, or encouragement only when a student needs it and in a way that helps.

That may sound like common sense, but I've seen teachers who give information that confuses students rather than making the material easier. I've also seen teachers who continue to give support when students don't need it, which results in students who are more dependent on the teacher. Remember, the goal is always to develop students who can learn without you beside them.

Ways to Scaffold Learning

Build a Strong Base

The first and most important way to scaffold learning is to help students build a strong foundation for the new information. I've built a stone garden in my yard this past summer. More accurately, my friend's son built it. I watched as he put the first layer of stone down, checked to see if it was level, then added sand and gravel to make the ground under the stone even so the first row was completely level. It took him much longer to do the bottom row than the top three rows. He explained to me that if the bottom wasn't right, none of the others will be. How true!

If our students don't have a sure footing when they start the lesson, they are less likely to catch up. Therefore, the first and most important thing you can do to scaffold learning is to help students *know what they already know* about a topic, or to build a context for them if they truly don't have one. We've talked about prior knowledge in other chapters, but it's so important I want to address it again. If you don't do anything else, you need to find out what students already know or think they know about the topic.

I was observing Mandy, a student teacher in a kindergarten classroom. She had spent a tremendous amount of time preparing her lesson, and she was nervous. She had chosen to read a book, which she introduced by saying, "Today we're going to read a book about farms. I want you to pay attention to what is on a farm, so we can talk about it when I finish." She turned to the third page, and David raised his hand. "That's not right. That's not what's on a farm." Confused, she told him to be quiet and kept reading. Robin was next, exclaiming, "I live on a farm, and we don't have a cow." As you can imagine, the lesson quickly went downhill. By the time I met Mandy in the conference room to discuss the lesson, she was in tears. As we talked through what had happened, she realized she had forgotten to find out what they already knew before she started.

The book showed what would be considered a typical farm, with cows, pigs, chickens, a tractor, and a farmer. But she was in an area where tobacco farming was the norm. Therefore, a farm had equipment and a farmer, but it didn't have animals. I explained that farming is one of those concepts that we think is common and simple but is actually complex. Just in North and South Carolina, we have tobacco farms, hog farms, peach farms, apple farms, and Christmas tree farms! If she had started the lesson by asking her students to describe things you find on a farm, she would have been able to talk about that there are different types of farms, and that today's story is about one type of farm.

Take it One Step at a Time

Another important strategy is to chunk learning into manageable portions and ensure understanding throughout the process. Think of new learning as climbing a staircase. You don't just jump to the top step; you climb the steps one at a time. Sequencing is a key part of this strategy. I have found this to be true with my graduate students when they write a research synthesis paper. Many of them say that they aren't too worried about it because they have written papers before. But it's a different type of research paper; they are to pull together only what other research says about their topic, and it is a challenging assignment. To ensure they are successful, I do four key things throughout each step of the process: modeling by showing them a finished product and detailing the steps; thinking out loud so they can understand the process and follow it rather than always needing me to do it for them; anticipating difficulties and warning them of potential pitfalls; and providing encouragement.

Every time I do this, a student questions whether or not this is a valuable use of class time. However, by the end of the class, the student always comes back and says, "I was wrong; this really helped me understand what I needed to do." A colleague asked me why I spend so much time teaching students how to do this assignment. In his words, "Can't they figure it out on their own? They are graduate students." I learned during my first semester that my students had never really written from a research perspective before graduate school. And, if I just gave them the assignment, they were frustrated and more likely to fail the project. If I'm going to have high expectations and provide rigorous assignments, I need to provide step-by-step guidance so they can be successful. This is true whether teaching graduate students or young children.

What's Good for One Must Be Good for All

There are times when a particular scaffolding strategy should be used
with everyone. That's true in my research project that I described earlier. If
you know that a concept or assignment will be difficult for everyone, you
should scaffold it for all students. But it's also important to individualize the
scaffolding depending on the needs of particular students.

One of my favorite examples is when I want students to write vivid descriptions. I place students in groups of three or four and give them a file
folder with a picture pasted on the outside. I also give each student a stack of
the tiny, one-by-one inch Post-it notes. I give them a short time to look at the
picture as a group (no talking yet) and then I allow one minute for students to
individually write as many words as possible to describe their picture. They
are to write one word per Post-it and get as many as possible written during
the minute (still no talking). Next, they talk together as a group about the picture and their words. They can sort their words, figure out any duplicates, or
whatever they want to do. After several minutes, I tell them they have to
write one sentence about their picture, using the words on the Post-its.

This immediately sparks comments, such as "I don't have a word I need!"
or "What about a period?" Depending on my purpose, this is a great opportunity to talk about grammar or punctuation. They can add other words and
punctuation on additional Post-it notes. As a group they create a sentence
and put the Post-its together in sentence form on the folder. Groups share
with everyone by displaying the sentence on the folder. Extra words are stuck
inside the folder. Now I move students back to an individual activity: Write a
paragraph about your picture. Some students immediately attack the task
and move on. But for students who need additional help, I've built in two
specific forms of scaffolding. First, when Raul says he doesn't know how to
start, he can copy the group sentence and add other sentences to it. Second,
when Abigail asks, "I don't know what else to write, can you help me?" she
can refer to a bank of words related to the picture: all the extra words inside
the folder. It's an easy way to provide the extra help needed for individual
students.

A Final Note

Scaffolding is a critical part of motivating students because it provides a sense of confidence through authentic success. Even though I haven't ridden a bike in several years, I know I could do it again today. The strong foundation of learning has instilled in me a sense of confidence and enthusiasm for that skill. But I also know what would have happened to me if I had not had the scaffolding from my dad. As a teenager, however, I made the mistake of trying to ride a motorcycle by myself. I didn't really know what I was doing. I thought it was just like riding a bike, so it wouldn't be that hard. One wreck, one hospital visit, and multiple stitches later, I said I'd never ride a motorcycle again. And I haven't. Today, if someone offered to teach me, my first thought would be, "I can't!" because I couldn't before. That's the difference and the long-term impact of scaffolding. But scaffolding should never be permanent. Only provide the necessary amount and type of scaffolding to your students that will help them succeed. If you provide too much help, or if you always provide help whether they need it or not, you foster dependence and undercut the ultimate goal: independence.

Summary

- Students experience frustration in the classroom. It is our job as teachers to provide enough support so that they can eventually be successful.
- The training wheels you provide for your students should be temporary verbal, visual, or physical resources that will help them during the formation, development, and enhancement of learning.
- Only provide scaffolding when a student truly needs it.
- You can begin teaching each new skill or concept by building a strong foundation and activating prior knowledge.
- Learning is like climbing a staircase: You have to have strong footing on each step to climb to the top. Make sure you break your content into manageable chunks, or steps, and frequently check for understanding.
- As a teacher you should constantly model for your students, anticipate difficulties that may arise during the learning cycle, and provide encouragement throughout the process.

- Often scaffolding is crucial for all students; however, sometimes you must individualize the level of support you are giving for each student depending on particular needs.
- Scaffolding is a critical part of building confidence in students because you are providing opportunities for authentic success.

If you would like more information...

This site helps teachers determine how to differentiate instruction: http://www.teach-nology.com/tutorials/teaching/differentiate/.

How to Differentiate Instruction in Mixed-Ability Classrooms, 2nd ed. by Carol Ann Tomlinson, ASCD.

Scaffolding Language, Scaffolding Learning: Teaching Second Language Learners in the Mainstream Classroom by Pauline Gibbon, Heinemann.

Scaffolding Learning by Jeffrey Wilhelm, Tanya Baker, Julia Dube, Heinemann.

Scaffolding Literacy Instruction: Strategies for the K–4 Classroom by Adrian Rodgers and Emily M. Rodgers, Heinemann.

T

Track Progress, Not Students

Don't mistake movement for achievement. It's easy to get faked out by being busy. The question is: Busy doing what?

Jim Rohn

Think About It...

How do students evaluate their own progress in your classroom?

Have you ever gotten so busy that you forgot what you were doing or why you were doing it? Our microwave, fast-food, anything-that-takes-lon-ger-than-two-minutes-is-bad attitude can undermine true progress. That's why I like Jim Rohn's comment. When I'm too busy, I realize that I have switched my focus from quality to quantity and have mistaken movement for achievement. Have you ever done that in your classroom? It is an important part of the learning process to pause and reflect on what we have done and how we have done it, or in a classroom, what we have learned and how we have learned it.

Learning something new can be frustrating. Most of us aren't perfect the first time we attempt something. And if we aren't careful, we give up before we truly begin. It's human nature to want to see progress quickly. Have you ever tried to lose weight? If so, you know how hard it is to think about losing 30 pounds. That seems so far away, and almost too much to attempt. So, we track progress weekly and celebrate the small steps such as losing five pounds or losing ten pounds. Why do we do that? Because tracking progress toward a larger goal helps us build a sense of competence and achievement, which leads to increased self-confidence, which then gives us courage to keep going. Take a look at the sample Confidence Cycle: That's the same cycle you want to build in your students.

We're going to specifically talk about tracking progress in learning, but the same principles apply to tracking other types of progress, such as behavior. You can do this formally or informally. Typically, we use formal indicators for measuring content knowledge and informal ones (if any) to track learning processes. However, you can blend the strategies together in a way that works best for you.

The Confidence Cycle

Keeping Track of *What I'm Learning*

Probably the most standard way of measuring progress in learning is through the use of pre- and post-tests. Pretests are typically given before you teach something, and post-tests are given after you complete your instruction. However, if you don't use the information from the pretest, why make students take it? One of my student teachers gave a pretest to his science class. All the students scored 90% or above. Then he taught a set of lessons about that content. His students were bored because they already knew the information. If you collect data about what your students know and don't know, then you should use the data to help you plan your instruction to best meet their needs. Otherwise you are just wasting time.

I visited Reid Ross Classical School in Fayetteville, North Carolina, and was impressed at the depth of commitment the teachers and students show toward tracking growth. They use weekly growth tests. The teachers were quick to tell me they would prefer to use a word other than test, but that's what they are now called. The growth tests are aligned with their curriculum and the accompanying pacing guide and serve as a tool for teachers to continually assess where their students' content knowledge. The short tests (10 minutes, once a week) provide two types of data for teachers. First, if most the class misses an item, the teacher knows it hasn't been taught effectively. Second, each teacher uses scores to diagnose individual students' needs for further instruction. More important, the students track their own growth weekly in a journal. Diane Antolak, principal at Reid Ross, notes that her experience as a marathon runner led to her idea for the growth tests. "If we track our progress physically and that helps us train better and more efficiently, why wouldn't we do that in learning also?"

It's not enough just to keep track of the numbers. You must use that information to improve learning. Kendra Alston, former teacher and now Academic Facilitator at Kennedy Middle School, also uses mini-assessments similar to the growth tests used at Reid Ross. If you look at Kendra's assessment (see page 144), you'll notice that immediately afterward she goes over the answers, and students must identify what items they missed and why. This shifts the focus from what they did wrong to what they are learning.

Informal Ways to Check for Understanding

Of course, you don't have to give a test to track learning. Many times, if you wait until the test to find out your students don't understand the content, it's too late for them to catch up. There are many informal ways to check for understanding. Exit slips, pieces of paper students must give you like a ticket out the door, are effective. At the end of class, simply ask them to write down the main thing they learned and a question they have. You can quickly scan the slips to see how much of the lesson stuck with them and what you need to reinforce the next day.

You can also wait until the next morning and have students write a short journal entry telling you the same information to use as a springboard for review. Or the journal can be used as a learning log. Every day at the end of class, students write down at least one thing they learned. By the end of the week, they have a list of at least five things they have learned, by the end of the month they have 20, and so on. This is more authentic than a test, and allows a student to see and personalize what they are learning.

Mini-Assessment

Name _____

Date of Test _____

Test Title _____

Summarize: What was this passage about?

Identify what you missed and why.

Make a list of what you missed. Place the number that fits beside each item.

1	I didn't understand the question.
2	I thought I had this right.
3	I studied this but forgot.
4	I have no clue about this.
5	I ran out of time and didn't try this.
6	I made a careless mistake.

Question I missed	I chose	Why	Correct answer

Keeping Track of *How I'm Learning*

A second important facet of measuring growth is to track improvement in the use of learning strategies. I did not do this well as a young teacher; but if I had my own classroom again, this would be a foundational part. Students need to think about how they learn and keep track of what works, what doesn't, and how that changes over time.

Kendra Alston does this exceptionally well with her students. She starts each year asking them to write about their favorite teacher. By analyzing the characteristics of those teachers, she is able to discover some of their *trigger points* for learning. Then she applies that knowledge in her own teaching to better connect with each student.

Next, she asks students to continually reflect on their learning in their *daybooks,* which are simple bound notebooks. Then she asks them to write a reflection on their learning at the end of the nine weeks. Although they wrote about specific content they learned, some of her students reflected on how they learn (see the example).

"Over this quarter, I've learned many things. One thing I've learned is teachers mean business and don't take kindly to slacking. I found that out the hard way. Another thing is that if you take the time to listen, teachers have a lot of helpful tips for passing the school year."

Justin, end of first nine weeks

"Something else that I learn [*sic*] would be about text organizers such as title, headings, caption/photograph, sidebars, and tags. Text organizers were not that confusing. At first I was getting tags and headings mixed up, but shortly I begin to understand them by the hands-on labs...I found that I understand the lessons better when we are able to do hands-on and get to experience and find what it is about ourselves."

Melissa, end of first nine weeks

"This school year has been unexplainable. I have improved so much over this past year I don't know where to begin...For once I actually worked hard on my work. Instead of waiting till the last minute to do work, I had to start right when it was given. I learned that the harder you work on an assignment, the more likely you will get a good grade."

Karina, end of year

How would your students respond if asked to write about their own learning? Would they agree with Justin that it's important to listen to teachers? Or might they identify with Melissa, who learns best by doing? Or do you have a Karina in your room, who realizes that working hard on an assignment results in a better grade? More important, what do you learn about yourself as a teacher when your students share comments such as these?

Keeping Track of Success

Another way to track progress is to have your students keep a *Victory List*. This can be in the back of their journals or student agendas; it just needs to be somewhere they can readily access it. A Victory List is simply a personal list of successes. It includes items such as

- I made a B on my paper.
- I drew a good picture.
- I didn't fight with Candace.
- I remembered that if I draw something, it helps me learn a new word.
- I took my paper home and Mom was proud of me.

The purpose of a victory list is to help us remember what we have accomplished, particularly when things aren't going so well.

I do this with my graduate students all the time. They come in to see me, worried about an assignment—particularly if there's a lot going on in their schools, and they are feeling pressed for time. After they finish talking, I remind them of all the other assignments they successfully completed, then I say, "I know you can do this one, too. After all, you did well on all the others, and they were also difficult. If you could do them, you can do this one, too." Sometimes when we're struggling, we forget all that we've accomplished. I especially like William Hurt's metaphor: You have to create a track record of breaking your own mold, or at least other people's idea of that mold.

Another purpose for a victory list is to help undo any failure messages in our heads. As we discussed, we remember losses far longer than we remember successes. Keeping a concrete list of successes is a constant visual reminder of progress.

Why Bother?

Blending formal and informal strategies to help students gauge their own progress toward goals develops a sense of confidence and competence in the classroom. We all achieve more when we can see step-by-step progress toward a goal. It doesn't matter if you use journals, tests, bookmarks, posters, a Web page, or some other form to chart growth; what matters is that you do it.

Try It!

What would you like to try? Use the grid to help you plan.

	Specific Strategy or Activity
Keeping Track of What I've Learned	
Keeping Track of How I Learn	
Keeping Track of Success	

Summary

- Focus on quality—not quantity—in the classroom.
- Help students track their progress toward a larger goal. This builds a sense of accomplishment which leads to self-confidence and motivation to continue.
- Use data from pre- and post-tests to measure your students' progress in learning, and use the information to improve learning.
- Don't wait until the test to realize that your students do not understand the content you are teaching; continuously check for understanding through informal assessments.
- Show students how they learn best. Help them keep track of the strategies that work for them.
- Point out small victories for each and every student—and have them keep track of them as a constant visual reminder of their successes.

If you would like more information...

This site contains information about student-led conferences and multiple links to additional resources: http://www.educationworld.com/a_admin/admin/admin112. shtml/.

The Results Field Book: Practical Strategies from Dramatically Improved Schools by Mike Schmoker, ASCD.

A School-Wide Approach to Student-Led Conferences: A Practitioner's Guide by Patti Kinney, Mary Beth Munroe, and Pam Sessions, National Middle School Association.

Student-Led Parent Conferences by Linda Pierce-Picciotto, Scholastic.

U

Understanding
at High Levels

A miracle has happened: The light of understanding has shone upon my pupil's mind and behold all things are changed.

Annie Sullivan (Helen Keller's teacher)

Have you ever worked with a student who didn't understand no matter what you did? I remember vividly when I taught fractions and decimals to my sixth-grade class. It was my first full-time teaching job, and I was hired to finish the school year after another teacher left in February. I was regularly reminded by everyone that "the test" was coming and that the score determined whether or not the students were placed in advanced classes on promotion to junior high. Their math skills were particularly lacking; and when I started to review decimals, it was clear they had no understanding of the concept. I backed up to reteach fractions and then build to decimals. The students were still confused. I still remember teaching nothing but decimals and fractions for about six weeks. I also remember running out of practice problems for them to work; there are only so many ways to add, subtract, multiply, and divide fractions and decimals.

As I look back, I was unprepared to deal with the variety of student needs. (Is anyone truly prepared to do that during their first year?) The more they didn't understand, the more practice I assigned. I laugh at myself now.

It's as if I decided, "If they don't understand, do it again, only more times!" Apparently I also thought repetition and memorization would help students learn. Unfortunately, for many students, that only leads to a surface understanding of content.

Demonstrating How Instead of What

A teacher in a recent workshop said when she wants to know that students really understand how to do something such as using prediction skills, she gives them something on the test they have never read before. Another teacher questioned that strategy, and it led to a great discussion. There are two issues here. First, if you want to test students on comprehension of specific content, the test should do that. But if you want to test them on use of strategies such as inference, addition, or reading a map, they should be able to apply that using a new text or situation.

Think about how that applies in life. How often do you have a test on what you read? Do you ever go to a party and hear this conversation: "Did you read today's paper? Really, what story did you read? What was the main idea? Who were the main characters? What happened? Can you provide supporting details for that?" It's more likely that you use the information you read in a conversation that was related to the story: "Oh, you're a stockbroker? In this morning's paper there was a story about the inflation rate. How do you think that will impact the stock market?"

In everyday life, we almost always use information to relate to something else. This is also true in most state curriculum standards. Although the standard may include knowledge of specific information, the focus usually is on using basic facts in an applied situation. Nevertheless, 90% of the time in school, we ask pretty basic questions. Scott Chambers, an eighth-grade student at Jay M. Robinson Middle School in Charlotte, North Carolina, described his school during a recent awards ceremony as "a place where learning is fun, not a drab building where you memorize facts but where you learn lessons that will carry you through life…. 'In education, we are striving not to teach youth to make a living but to make a life.' One of my favorite teachers impressed the importance of critical thinking skills versus the memorization of facts and figures. After all, we have the Internet for that. Critical thinking prepares us to compete in the global market. It will be these lessons that I take to high school and college."

Questioning at Higher Levels of Understanding

I think understanding is like climbing a mountain. You may have to start at the bottom, but to get the full view you have to get to the top. You get to the top one step at a time. The steps become increasingly more difficult as you go, but the view is worth it. There are many models for organizing higher levels of questions, but I find two especially helpful and practical. Each takes a slightly different approach and can be adapted for your precise purposes.

Short, Simple, and to the Point

Taffy Raphael created a four-level hierarchy for questioning that is easy to use and remember. *Right there* questions refer to questions at the most basic or literal level, those that can be answered by looking right in the text material. These are the questions that tend to be asked most often in classrooms, and they are rarely asked in life or on standardized tests. *Think and search* questions require the student to think about the given information and pull from several parts of that information to determine a correct response. *On my own* questions ask students to relate the material to their own lives through evaluation; and *Author and me* questions require one to apply this information to a new or different situation.

Raphael Hierarchy for Questioning

	Right There	Think and Search	Author and Me	On My Own
English	In a Midsummer Night's Dream, who did Hermia love?	Give examples of how Shakespeare incorporates elements of humor into his play.	Why do you think Puck enjoyed causing trouble for the humans?	What would you do if you were forbidden from dating the person you love?
Math	What is the Pythagorean Theorem?	Explain the relationship between a sine and cosine wave.	Can you identify various geometric shapes you see in nature?	Design the perfect container to sell M&M's. What shape bag or box will be the most marketable, yet cost effective?
Science	What function does the mitochondrion of a cell serve?	Paraphrase the process of mitosis.	Relate what you have read about the characteristics of the cell vacuole to a balloon.	What are your thoughts on stem cell research?
History	What is socialism?	Compare and contrast communism to democracy.	Based on what you've read about the types of government, which type does our school most resemble?	If you could begin a new government on an isolated island, what type(s) of government would you choose? Why?

A Matrix for Questioning

Kathy Bumgardner, the reading specialist for Gaston County Schools, North Carolina, introduced me to the Question Matrix illustrated in the sample. This grid crosses basic questions (who, what, when, where, why, and how) with verbs (is, did, can, would, will, and might) to create a matrix that addresses all levels of questioning. If you divide the grid into four quadrants, you'll notice the upper left addresses basic questions; and the closer you go to the bottom right, the higher the level of the question.

I've used the grid to help me create questions for leading a class discussion; but I prefer to copy the grid on bright colors of card stock. I cut the squares apart, and put one complete set in a plastic bag. After my students have read a portion of text material, I put them in small groups, and give each group a bag. In turn, each student draws a card and has to finish the question. For example, if I draw the question card *how would*, I might ask, "How would you react if you were in the same situation as the main character?" Then, the rest of the group must answer the question. I've done this with hundreds of teachers, and you can use these questions with almost any topic. It's also a great way to review before a test.

Question Matrix

What Is	When Is	Where Is	Which Is	Who Is	Why Is	How Is
What Did	When Did	Where Did	Which Did	Who Did	Why Did	How Did
What Can	When Can	Where Can	Which Can	Who Can	Why Can	How Can
What Would	When Would	Where Would	Which Would	Who Would	Why Would	How Would
What Will	When Will	Where Will	Which Will	Who Will	Why Will	How Will
What Might	When Might	Where Might	Which Might	Who Might	Why Might	How Might

Focusing on Problem Solving

Encouraging higher levels of understanding shifts the focus to solving problems. Rather than simply learning about map skills, we learn how to use that information to plan a trip. We learn how to spell and write correctly so we can communicate clearly and effectively to others and not just for the sake of knowing how. You can take almost any concept you need to teach and frame it in a practical way.

One of the most effective ways to do this is to let the students generate ideas as to how the information could be used to solve problems. You may need to facilitate some questions; but when you do this, you are not only encouraging problem solving, you are giving them an immediate practice opportunity. I've been in many classrooms where students asked a question, and the teacher said something like, "That's a great question for homework. Everyone see what you can come up with and we'll talk about it again tomorrow." When you do that, besides providing a problem-solving opportunity, you encourage independence and ownership in learning.

Finding Information

Anatole France said, "An education isn't how much you have committed to memory, or even how much you know. It's being able to differentiate between what you know and what you don't." I would add that education is also about knowing where to find the information you don't know. Facts are important, but facts alone don't guarantee or measure understanding.

Several years ago I heard a speaker discussing the information overload in our information-rich society. He said that the amount of information available to us doubles every 24 hours, and the amount available would only increase in the future. With the Internet, e-mail, and other electronic databases, the amount of available information is unbelievable. A critical skill for the future is the ability to find information.

Teaching students to research a topic can begin early. Even primary-age children can generate questions and look for answers. Those activities are the basics of doing research. Then, teachers can move students into more formal research assignments. Follow the same process you would with any type of new knowledge: Build on prior knowledge and help students set their own goals for learning, show them models of what a *good* finished product looks like, chunk the steps in the process, and provide multiple opportunities for feedback and revision.

Assessing Understanding

Giving students opportunities to answer high-level questions or to do activities at higher levels of understanding is not enough. Once I was in the classroom of a friend who asked me provide feedback on her questioning skills. She was intentional about asking high levels of questions, but I was surprised that she accepted basic answers to those questions, rather than pushing her students to expand their answers. When she and I talked about what I saw, she said, "That's what is not working. I thought it was my questions, but I see that it's the answers or lack of answers that is the problem." She quickly adjusted her instruction to include more open-ended follow-up questions, and her students flourished.

You may also need to adjust your wait time, the amount of time you give students to answer a questions. Researchers observing classes tend to find that teachers do not allow as much time for students to answer as they think they do. That may be because it simply seems like it is longer when you and your students are waiting for an answer. A good gauge is to allow at least double the time you think you should wait. For those who want a more definitive range, allow a minimum of three seconds for students to answer your questions.

Finally, as you move your students into more complex work, you may find that they need more support and encouragement. A part of the process will be making mistakes, and it's important that students learn from those mistakes. After all, isn't that what education is really about? R. Buckminster Fuller agrees: "If I ran a school, I'd give the average grade to the ones who gave me all the right answers, for being good parrots. I'd give the top grades to those who made a lot of mistakes and told me about them, and then told me what they learned from them."

Summary

- Although comprehension and the ability to recall information is important, it is even more crucial to teach students how to apply the information they have acquired to new situations.

- A variety of questions should be included in each discussion and lesson you teach. Students need to begin with concrete, lower-level questions but be directed to move toward higher-order thinking through the questions you pose. There are several guides that help teachers scaffold questions from literal to interpretive and then to global thinking.

- Rather than being a keeper of all knowledge, encourage students to take ownership of their learning and solve problems independently with critical thinking skills.

- Today's informational society demands that we teach students how to successfully locate the knowledge they need. Teaching the *how* has become more important than the *what.*

- To truly assess understanding, your questioning techniques must be carefully planned out.

If you would like more information...

This site contains the new and revised Bloom's taxonomy: http://www.apa.org/ed/new_blooms.html/.

This site contains question stems for Bloom's taxonomy: http://www.kcmetro.cc.mo.us/longview/ctac/blooms.htm/.

A Taxonomy for Learning, Teaching, and Assessing: A Revision of Bloom's Taxonomy of Educational Objectives edited by Lorin W. Anderson and David R. Krathwohl, Allyn & Bacon.

Improving Classroom Questions, Second Edition by Kenneth R. Chuska, Phi Delta Kappa International.

Teaching Question-and-Answer Relationship Revisited by Taffy Raphael, The Reading Teacher.

V

Variety Is the Spice of Life

I hear and I forget. I see and I remember. I do and I understand.

Confucius

Think About It...

If you were to write a recipe for the perfect class, what would it be?

One challenge teachers face is that when we find something that works, we want to stick with it all the time. The truth is that students need a balance of predictability and variety. Having basic routines and structures is critical, but there is a difference between having those routines and just doing the same things every day. Let's go back to what we talked about with student engagement. A good, basic classroom routine is to have something for students to do when they enter your classroom. Some teachers have something on the board, overhead, or on each student's desk. But if you have exactly the same thing every day, students soon become bored. In my classroom I found that it was important to have something up on the board for them to do, but I should change the type of something periodically.

Balancing routines with variety, that's the trick. Think about going to a circus: You expect to see clowns, lions and tigers, and acrobats. But you are

157

amazed when something happens you aren't expecting. At its best teaching is like a circus; it has variety and excitement.

Think About It...

How much variety is in your class recipe?

Multiple Intelligences Theory

The 1983 release of Dr. Howard Gardner's book, *Frames of Mind: The Theory of Multiple Intelligences,* sparked a new round of discussions about how we learn. Challenging the notion that intelligence is the same for everyone and can be measured through and intelligence quotient (IQ) test, Dr. Gardner contends intelligence is more complex, and there are different ways that one can be intelligent. He describes eight types of intelligence, which are outlined in the Multiple Intelligences table. We can use this information to connect with students in new and increasingly effective ways.

Multiple Intelligences

Linguistic	Learns best through words/language
Logical-Mathematical	Learns best through logic and/or numbers
Spatial	Learns best through visuals or pictures
Musical	Learns best through rhythms and/or music
Intrapersonal	Learns best through self-reflection and/or individually
Bodily-Kinesthetic	Learns best through physical activity
Interpersonal	Learns best through social interaction
Naturalist	Learns best through experiences in nature

I talked with a teacher who interpreted this to mean you should find out each student's type of intelligence, and then only teach lessons to the student in a way that matches that intelligence. That seems limiting and impractical for today's classrooms. Instead, incorporating activities that address various intelligences allows students to construct deeper knowledge by seeing the concept through the different intelligence lenses. For example, I may be a linguistic learner, but my knowledge of geography is enhanced through visuals (spatial). So although you may want to provide instruction individually tailored to a student's intelligence(s), also plan lessons for all students that incorporate elements of the different intelligences.

Sample Activities for Multiple Intelligences

	Science	Math
Verbal/Linguistic	Create a diary on "A Water Droplet's Journey Through the Water Cycle" (from the water droplet's perspective)	Give verbal directions to a peer on steps to solve a problem
Logical/Mathematical	Find four different ways to classify a collection of rocks	Calculate unknown angles in a polygon
Visual/Spatial	Pretend you are food particle & can travel through the digestive system	Estimate measurements by sight & by touch
Body/Kinesthetic	Become, and act out the major organs of the body	Physically become a number line to understand the concept of negative and positive
Musical/Rhythmic	Make up a song to remember the order of the planets	Learn mathematical operations through songs, jingles, and rhythmic beats
Naturalist	Classify different foods for healthy diet planning	Find examples of triangles, octagons, parallelograms, etc…in nature
Interpersonal	Work in groups for labs or activities	Become experts on a topic and teach it to your classmates
Intrapersonal	Journal topic: "If I could be any animal I would be a…"	Think about how you learn math best and record which strategies seem to work best for you

*Questions adapted from: http://www.multi-intell.com/MI_chart.html

Missy Miles, a teacher at Jay M. Robinson Middle School, wrote *A Recipe for a Successful Classroom*. Notice how it incorporates many of the intelligences, along with a healthy dose of student choice.

A Recipe for a Successful Classroom

1	tablespoon of lecture (for auditory learners)
2	cups of small-group discussion of any sort of variety
½	cup of guided reading
1½	cups of hands-on activities
½	cups of various activities that involve movement. Sprinkle in little by little, not all at once.
3	tablespoons of music and art, which integrate content material
2	cups of opportunity for students to decide how they will be assessed
4	ounces of graphic organizers

The more you stir and allow these ingredients to blend, the more productive your recipe will be. Allow adequate time to let ideas, questions, and exploration occur before putting in the oven to brown.

Differentiated Instruction: Does Differentiation Mean Difficulty?

Differentiated instruction (DI) is a concept offered as an alternative to ability grouping, and I hear many interpretations of what it means. For most it means creating lessons that include different elements to meet the needs of each individual student in a diverse classroom. According to the technical definition, in DI a teacher varies the content (what), process (how), or product (demonstration of learning) of instruction to enhance student understanding. One concern I hear from some teachers is that differentiation means some students will miss some learning. In sports, there are basic warm-up exercises and drills that every player does. But good coaches work with each players during practice to also to increase strengths and strengthen any weaknesses. That is how I view differentiation: Cover core information with everyone, but adjust the content as needed, vary how it is taught, and assess that content to help everyone learn the most on an individual basis.

Varying the *What*

Varying the content does not mean ignoring your content standards, but it does mean paying attention to the students' prior knowledge. In fact, I'd argue that a lockstep approach to standards, using a *one-size-fits-all* approach to content sets up a hierarchy in which the standards are elevated to a higher level than your students. Given the diversity that exists in most of our classrooms today, such an approach doesn't meet anyone's needs. When you take time to determine what your students already know about a subject and adjust the content accordingly, your students learn more, not less. Sometimes, you have a student who already knows the material. Other times, students need additional instruction and background knowledge before they can understand the new concept. Differentiating content means not forcing someone to wait through content they have mastered while you are assisting others in a review detour.

In my classroom, I layered meaning with texts, moving from an easier text to more challenging text. I was explaining this in a workshop when a high school English teacher came up afterward. She explained that she uses this exact process with individual students who struggle with complex literature selections. Instead of using the junior versions of literature that are available commercially, she teaches her students to use *Cliff's Notes,* not instead of reading, but to help organize the reading and support their understanding. One of my graduate students also uses this strategy with her at-risk classes. She actually rewrites every chapter in her text, streamlining the content and making it easier to read. Students start with that study guide, then read the textbook; and they are much more successful.

Varying the *How*

Allowing students to have choices in how they learn can increase involvement, ownership, and overall understanding. Some of your students learn best by listening, others by doing something. Highly effective classrooms tend to use a mix of activities that appeal to different learning modalities.

First, you can vary groupings. Some students work well individually, others prefer small groups, and still others learn effectively during whole class instruction. You can also vary how the material is presented: verbally, visually, or in a way that allows students to construct their own knowledge by creating something. Use your knowledge of multiple intelligences as you develop lesson plans including activities such as those in the sample.

In an ideal classroom, every lesson would be uniquely tailored to each individual student. However, in the real world, recognize that your students learn better in different ways, and mix varying elements throughout the lesson. Focus on activities to match the intelligences of your students and the *how* is much easier.

Varying the *Result*

Finally, you can vary the product of learning, or how students demonstrate they understood the material. For me, this is the easiest place to differentiate for each student. Let everyone's imagination run wild as you plan and design your assessments in this area. Rather than requiring everyone to turn in reports, allow each student to summarize information in a format of his or her choice. It may be in the form of a PowerPoint presentation, model, video, poem, or song. To ensure consistency in quality while allowing for flexibility of the type of product, use a clear rubric.

Differentiation in Action

Christy Holloway incorporates differentiation in her sixth-grade math classroom through the use of learning centers:

> The basis of the differentiation I do in my classroom begins with the way I set my students up in groups. Students are placed in groups of four. Each desk contains a number one through four, [based on the students' achievement levels]. It also helps me to set up centers so that I can control what types of activities each child participates in during center time.
>
> I set up seven centers around the room. At each center there are four different folders, with a number (one through four). When it is center time, if a child sits at a one in his or her group, then he or she may choose a center and complete the activity in folder number one at that center. If a child sits at the three spot in his or her group, then during center time he or she may choose a center and complete the activity in the folder number three at that center.
>
> When preparing activities for each center, I make sure that the concept for all four folders is the same. For example, at center number one, everyone may be working on concepts that involve order of operations. However, the level of difficulty varies based on the folder number. Folders one and two are basic activities, and folders three and four are enrichment activities. This arrangement allows me to challenge the higher level students and

do some remediation for the lower level students. Some centers are set up so that ones and fours work together and twos and threes work together. Although my ones and twos are low, I still want to challenge them. Therefore, on challenging activities, I pair them with the higher-performing students so that they can help and support each other.

Christy incorporates elements of varying the what and varying the how through learning centers to enhance learning for her students. But she also varies the what when she assigns homework. "Another way I differentiate using the number system is with my homework assignments. I write homework on the board by seat numbers. Ones and twos usually have the same assignments, and threes and fours have the same assignment. The number of problems is always very close to the same, but the type and difficulty level is different. Higher-level students should not simply be doing more problems; they should be doing enrichment-type problems." Christy's instruction incorporates the essence of differentiated instruction, providing variety so that each student learns.

Summary

- Although structure and routine are critical parts of a successful classroom, students thrive off of variety.

- If you plan lessons that incorporate elements of multiple intelligences, students can learn and acquire knowledge in different ways.

- One size does not fit all. Given the diversity that exists in classrooms today, differentiation is crucial. Teach the core information to everyone, but adjust the content as needed and vary assessments to get the most out of each student.

- If you tailor reading assignments to individual abilities, you may need to have several texts for one lesson to accommodate the wide range of reading levels in your classroom.

- Students learn in many different ways—it is important that you reach all of them. Vary your teaching style.

- Students should have ownership in how they demonstrate knowledge. Give them choice on the format of their assessments.

If you would like more information...

This site connects specific learning styles to teaching strategies: http://www.berghuis.co.nz/abiator/lsi/lsiframe.html/.

A plethora of informative Web sites on learning styles and multiple intelligences: http://www.kn.sbc.com/wired/fil/pages/list multiplega.html#cat2/.

The following two Web sites explore all about multiple intelligences: http://www.multi-intell.com/MI_chart.html and http://www. mcmel.org/erica.mi/mainpage.html/.

The Differentiated Classroom: Responding to the Needs of All Learners by Carol Ann Tomlinson, ASCD.

Multiple Intelligences in the Classroom, 2nd Edition by Thomas Armstrong, ASCD.

So Each May Learn: Integrating Learning Styles and Multiple Intelligences by Matthew J. Perini, Harvey F. Silver, and Richard W. Strong, ASCD.

W

What You See
Is What You Get

For the great majority of mankind are satisfied with appearance as though they were realities and are often more influenced by the things that seem than by those that are.

Niccolo Machiavelli

Advertisers spend approximately $12 billion per year marketing specifically to kids. They know that kids, like everyone else, are influenced by what they see. This is also true in your classroom, where students are particularly influenced by three things that they see:

1. You as the teacher
2. The physical environment
3. Other role models

Think About It...

What three words would your students use to describe you?

Teacher as Personal Model

Have you ever thought of yourself as a model? Models walk down a runway, and everyone around them looks at them and scrutinizes every move they make. That is also true for teachers. You are the most important image your students see every day at school. They notice what you wear, what you do, what you read, and whether you are sick or feeling well. I'm not talking about whether or not you have a quiet or bubbly personality; I'm saying they notice whether you smile when you see them, or if you look upset every time they ask a question.

Erin Owens, a first grade teacher, tells me, "Each day, no matter what I am going through personally or professionally, I try to display as much enthusiasm as possible. How do you expect students to embrace learning and become lifelong learners if you do not? Many times, my actions and attitude toward academics impact my students more than discussions." Every one of your students watches and learns from you. The question is, what do they learn?

One of my graduate students hit an unexpected obstacle with an assigned project for my class. To implement an interdisciplinary unit the other teachers on his teaching team needed to cooperate. His motivation was higher because he would receive a grade for the project. He reluctantly told me that to get everyone to participate he had to do his unit on the theme of Cinderella. As a math teacher, and frankly as a male, this would have been about his last choice for a teaching unit. But he was stuck with it. When he finished the unit, he shared a story about his experience.

Several of his students who were also on his football team told him they had learned a lot in the unit, but they mostly learned that sometimes you have to do things you don't want to do. They said they knew he didn't want to teach about Cinderella (he ultimately had the students create a budget for a mock production), but he still made it fun. And *that* they remembered! He modeled two specific life lessons for his students: persistence in spite of obstacles and the importance of keeping a positive attitude even when you don't want to do something.

Teachers should be great models of lifelong learning. Do your students see you still learning and growing? Do you tell or show them new things you learned in a workshop or from a book? Do your students ever see you reading?

Teachers also model caring, particularly by showing an interest in students outside of the classroom. Have you seen a child's face light up when you crossed paths at the grocery store and spoke? Or when you attended a game, birthday party, play, or concert? I hear countless stories of students who thrive in a particular teacher's classroom and how that sparked when the teacher showed an interest in their personal lives.

One way to connect with your students is through writing. A principal at a local school told me she sends home a personal, handwritten letter to all students in the summer before the start of the school year. Many of her students wrote back, and almost all of them came to see her at the start of the year to thank her. Tracie Clinton (Cotton Belt Elementary) mails postcards home to her students so they can "see how proud I am of them, and I want them to be proud of themselves. This small effort on my part seems to build their self-esteem. A parent of a little girl I had last year stopped me over the summer and told me that her daughter was so touched by the card I had sent her in the mail. She loved it so much she actually slept with it under her pillow at night. This touched me so greatly!" It doesn't matter how you connect, just do it!

Teacher Modeling of Strategies

It's also important to model what good learning looks like for your students. Think-alouds are a critical part of every teacher's repertoire. When you *think aloud* you're simply verbally explaining what you are thinking. Many students simply have no idea of the processes used when learning new information. They see learning as the unbreakable code because they don't have the key. What we know as teachers is that there are multiple steps that go into any learning process and one step toward breaking that down for our students is by modeling our thinking. It's so simple we assume everyone else knows how to talk through that process. Your strong students do that in their heads, but your struggling students do not understand it. That's why it's important to model your thinking for students.

Physical Environment

What does your room say about your instruction? The look or appearance indicates how your classroom works, both good and bad.

When I was assigned to teach the at-risk classes in my school, I knew I needed to send a message the moment the kids stepped in the room. Unfortunately, it was common knowledge who was assigned to the *developmental* class because of low test scores. Most of my students came in with a negative attitude, and I was determined to change that perception. Instead of a dumping ground (the typical view of the low-level classes), I wanted them to see an exciting and fun class that was attractive to all students. I took the entire back wall, put up three bulletin board backdrops with bright borders, such as blue and yellow, and I put catchy headings, such as *Spotlight on....* These were empty until the year started, then they were continually filled with student work that I rotated regularly. I wanted to send two messages to my students. First, it's a new year and we all start with a blank slate. Second, in this class it's all about your learning.

I used visuals throughout the room, probably to the extreme. No space was left unfilled. I had pictures, lists, vocabulary words, and charts (my naïve attempt at the current recommended word wall) on the other walls and bulletin boards. One time I posted spelling words on the ceiling just to see if my students would notice. Another time I wrote trivia questions about the state symbols on balloons and hung them from the ceiling (that was before the fire marshal said it wasn't allowed). The answers were inside the balloons, which both intrigued and frustrated my students. I also had posters with inspirational quotes around. Based student response I knew my classroom was a place that everyone wanted to visit; it was exciting and fun and not the dumb kids' room.

Posting Student Work

As you think about your classroom, you want the walls and other physical spaces to contain items in three categories. First and foremost, you should have plenty of space to share the student work. You can use the walls as I did; or you might use space in the hallway outside your classroom or near the office to showcase special work. I spoke to a middle school principal; his technical education classes built display cases for the school, and each month they rotated sample projects from the art classes. It was a great way to focus attention on work outside the core subject areas. I've been in several classrooms lately where teachers put volleyball net up across the back of the room, so they could use clothespins to post sample work products. That's an easy way to frequently change the postings.

Posting Key Information

The second type of material to display is key information students need regularly. For example, if there are seven steps for every laboratory experiment, why not post them so students can refer to it if needed? Or the steps of the writing process? Or key resources for doing research? Simple reminders, particularly posted while students are trying to learn the steps, can be helpful. It doesn't excuse them from learning the process, but it can minimize disruptions that occur when one student forgets. It's also an invaluable tool for new students and substitute teachers.

When I observe student teachers, they typically start a lesson by telling students to turn to a certain page in a book. Then as they start to teach, multiple students will interrupt to ask for the page number. Afterward, we discuss ways to improve the lesson, and I typically suggest writing the page number on the board. Then if students ask or say they didn't hear you the first time, you can simply point to the information on the board, which cuts down on the interruptions to the lesson.

Think About It...

What key information should be posted in your room? What reference information is helpful?

Posting Inspirational Quotes

Third, posting inspirational quotes and posters is a wonderful way to remind students to focus on success. In Sylvia White's room at Reid Ross Classical School, the quote on the chalkboard caught my eye. When I asked her about it, her students quickly chimed in to explain that she puts an inspiring quote up every day. They were able to state several of their favorite quotes and explain what each meant. There are many sources for quotes, particularly on the Internet, and it's easy to find ones that are pertinent to your students.

Role Models

The final area of appearance is that of role models. In Chapter G, Goals and Success, I discussed the importance of role models as mentors, but in this section let's focus on the messages students receive from the people they see in your classroom, real persons as well as characters in books.

Erin Owens explains that in her first grade classroom, "I bring many different people from the community into my room: Junior Achievement executives, high school helpers, Winthrop (local university) interns, district office employees to read, professors dressed as Abe Lincoln, and (other) volunteers. Each of these visitors stresses the need to work hard in school. They all maintain high expectations for the class and serve as role models." Notice the variety of visitors in her classroom, but all of them model high expectations for learning.

Models in Text Materials

Similarly, you probably have people come into your classroom, and I'm sure you think about the kind of role models they are. But there are also less obvious ways we send students messages about who or what they can be. One of these subtle ways of communicating role expectations is through the images students see in their reading. When I worked for a textbook company, we were required by one school district in Florida to provide a grid that listed every selection in the reading book. In the chart we had to list whether the main character was a male or female, the ethnicity of all characters, and whether there was a character with special needs. At first I thought it was a tedious request, but I quickly saw the value.

Even though publishers have responded by printing books that are more reflective of our society, too often our instructional materials don't speak to particular groups of your students. Textbooks and other books are more inclusive than in the past, but it is still difficult to find the balance we might like. Just last month a teacher shared her struggle to find a historical novel to use in an after-school book club for girls. She specifically wanted the book to have an African American girl as a main character, and in all the books she found the girls were slaves.

After two weeks, she finally found a historical novel about a friendship between two girls. As she described it to me, she wanted her students to read historical fiction, but she didn't want them to think that all African Americans were slaves. "It's a part of history, but only a part." That's why it's important to pay attention to who your students read about or research. In another case I heard a student ask, "Are all scientists boys? Does that mean I can't be a scientist?" The teacher was quick to say no and found several examples to share with the young girl.

As you build your classroom library, find books that are reflective of your students' interests, but that also include positive role models. If your students like basketball and are always talking about the National Basketball Association (NBA), find biographies for players who are true role models, both on and off the court. (Grant Hill is one of my favorites.) Be intentional about research. Find people in history that are true role models, and share them with your students. If your school has a character education program, you can easily link this to that curriculum, but if not you can chose the people you talk about and read about in your classroom.

Providing a range of role models throughout your content requires an investment of your time and energy, but the benefits are substantial. For some of your students, the best role models in their lives are those they encounter in your classroom. And, to paraphrase Machiavelli, some of your students accept what they see as though it is reality, because they are often influenced by what things appear to be rather than what they are.

Summary

- Your students are experts at reading you. Try to display enthusiasm and sincerity every moment of every day.
- Teachers are the best models of lifelong learning.
- Caring can be modeled for your students by taking a genuine interest in their lives.
- Think-alouds and other strategies model what learning looks like.
- The physical environment of you classroom should convey an inviting, positive message from the moment your students walk through the door. Display student work, key reference information, and inspirational quotes and posters.
- Students benefit from role models; make a conscious effort to provide a wide variety for your class.

If you would like more information…

This site provides tips for decorating your classroom: http://schoolsupplies.lifetips.com/cat/60150/classroom-decorations/.

Creating an Inviting Classroom Environment by Elizabeth S. Foster-Harrison and Ann Adams-Bullock, Phi Delta Kappa International.

Improving Comprehension With Think Aloud Strategies by Jeffery D. Wilhelm, Ph.D., Scholastic.

The Inviting School Treasury by William Watson Purkey and Paula Helen Stanley, Brookcliff Publishers.

X-Factor

You have to take care of yourself before you can take care of others.

Old Saying

Too often, I talk to teachers who have lost their motivation. They are overwhelmed by paperwork, frustrated with discipline problems, and feel as though no one values their expertise—evidenced by the fact that they are *told* more than they are *asked*. We'll talk more about these issues in Chapter Y, You Are the Key, but now I want to focus on how to pull yourself up when you feel defeated or unmotivated. This is crucial, because your level of motivation will be directly related to your students' levels of motivation, and vice versa.

Several weeks ago I received an e-mail from teacher who was completely at the end of her rope. When her students returned from the winter break, they were unfocused and disruptive. Her classroom routines, which had been effective before the break, weren't working anymore. She was having trouble starting her class, and by the time she e-mailed me, she was questioning her skills as a teacher. Sometimes you feel like you are sinking slowly in quicksand and going under, but there's nothing you can do about it. All you need is someone to throw you a line to help you hang on. That's exactly what I did with her, but how can you prevent stress from driving you that far down?

You can stop the negative before you sink too far, but you must focus on yourself. There's an old saying: You can't take care of others until you take care of yourself. I was reminded of that on a recent flight. A young boy traveling alone was seated near me, and the flight attendant reminded me that if the oxygen masks dropped from the ceiling because of a lack of pressure, I needed to place a mask on myself before I placed one on him. To help our students, we must take care of ourselves.

Taking care of ourselves means taking time to rest, getting enough exercise, and having balance in our lives. But it also means being inspired about who we are and what we do. There are seven key ways I incorporate inspiration in my life.

Incorporating Inspiration

> 1. Build a positive memory file
> 2. Read books that inspire
> 3. Watch inspirational movies
> 4. Find everyday heroes
> 5. Surround yourself with motivating thoughts
> 6. Keep a success journal
> 7. Make the choice every day

Build a Positive Memory File

You've probably received a thank you note, a card, or a picture drawn by a student. Did you save it? I kept a file folder in my desk with those and other reminders of times students gave me positive feedback. I remember one time it was just a scrap of paper with a smile drawn on it given to me by one of my most mischievous students. My first teaching job after graduation was with sixth graders. I still have a note from Tara, who mailed me a letter thanking me for being such a good teacher and helping her learn.

Start today building a memory file with pictures, e-mails, notes, or anything that acknowledges the good work you do as a teacher. Then on those days when things get tough, go to your file and look through it. You'll be surprised at how much it will cheer you up. You have these memories in your head; but when you are under a lot of stress, they're hard to remember. Keep these cues handy, so you can be reminded of your impact instantly. In my office I have a children's book about a farm. If you push the buttons on the side of the book, it talks (when you push the cow, it says, "cow" and then you hear a cow mooing). I love it because a student in a research class gave it to me. I was teaching my students how to write a synthesis of research, and I continually hammered the point that an author says something, rather than a book saying something, which is a common mistake.

My students laugh when I say, "A book can't say anything; a book can't talk." Karl brought me this book to show me that a book *can* talk. When I'm having a rough day and correcting the fifteenth paper with "according to the book," I look at my farm book, smile, and realize that I do get through to my students! What is in your memory file? Where do you keep those tangible memories so you can access them when you need some motivation?

Read Books That Inspire You

When I was teaching, I kept a copy of *The Thread That Runs So True* on my desk. It is Jesse Stuart's true story of his teaching career. I originally read it because my dad told me to read it, but I reread it because it taught me of all the power of being a teacher. The reason I kept it on my desk and read selected portions regularly was because it reminded me that on my toughest day, it could be worse. Jesse Stuart stumbled into being a teacher after accidentally going into the wrong room at his high school. Instead of his regular class, the room was being used to administer the teacher's exam; so he took the test and passed.

Then he asked to be placed in the one-room school where his sister taught. She left her job after she was beaten by one of the students. When he started he faced the same challenge: a 16-year-old first grader who believed this was *his* school and no teacher would tell him what to do. To keep his job Jesse had to fight the student after school, help bandage the hurt student, and clean up the blood because there was no custodian. Although I would never condone fighting with a student, this story provides a dual metaphor for me.

No matter how bad things were in my school, I never had to physically fight a student to keep my job. By the end of my second year of teaching, however, I realized that every teacher has to fight to do the job effectively; you may have to fight paperwork, unmotivated students, or your own feelings of frustration and depression. *The Thread That Runs So True* inspires me to recognize that everyone has to fight, and the fight can take you to a different level of teaching. You probably have books that inspire you. Keep a list of those in the back of your success journal, which we'll talk about later in the chapter.

Watch Movies That Inspire You

I also love watching movies about teachers and students to be reminded that teachers make a difference. My favorite two movies are older; *Conrack,* Pat Conroy's story of his teaching experiences on an island off the South Carolina coast, and *The Sound of Music,* in which a nontraditional teacher taught children in one family about music and life.

My new favorite is *The Emperor's Club,* which I saw at one of the lowest points in my university teaching career. A student plagiarized a project. That may be pretty typical these days, but this one was personal. The student was my advisee, and I was supervising her final project. I questioned my teaching, the standard I had set, and whether or not I had been a positive role model. I was tired, I was defeated, and I questioned my overall effectiveness as a university teacher. One of my colleagues recommended I see the movie; so one afternoon I stumbled into the theatre, still frustrated that somehow I had let this student down.

The movie was cathartic. In *The Emperor's Club* Kevin Kline plays a private school teacher who deals with a similar issue with his students. I won't spoil the movie for you if you haven't seen it, but pick it up on your next trip to the video store. It profiles a situation with students competing for a prize, then the movie fast forwards a number of years when Kevin Kline realizes that the student made a choice; and it really was the student's choice, not his. It was an epiphany for me; I cried through the last half of the movie. The powerful message still resonates with me: As teachers, we have tremendous positive influence over our students, but there are limitations to that influence. Students can and do make their own way, sometimes because of our influence, and sometimes despite our influence. And the joy and sorrow of teaching is exactly that; we do all we can do, and sometimes our hearts break.

Inspiring Movies for Teachers

True Stories of Teachers

Dangerous Minds	The story of Louanne Johnson, former marine, teaching English in an inner-city school
The Miracle Worker	A classic profile of Annie Sullivan and Helen Keller
Music of the Heart	The story of Roberta Guaspari, a single mother who moves to Harlem and becomes a violin teacher
Stand and Deliver	Profiles Jaime Escalante's teaching in an inner city Los Angeles school

Other Inspiring Movies for Teachers

Mr. Holland's Opus	Richard Dreyfuss as a musician and composer who teaches music
Dead Poet's Society	Robin Williams as unconventional teacher in a private school
Finding Forrester	Sean Connery as a writer who teaches a young man about life
Up the Down Staircase	The story of an idealistic new teacher in an urban high school
Sister Act 2: Back in the Habit	Whoopi Goldberg as a "nun" working with students in a Catholic school

Movies About Coaches as Teachers

Hoosiers	Based on the true story of a small Indiana basketball team, their new coach, and their journey to a championship
Remember the Titans	Based on the true story integration at T.C. Roberson High School as seen through the story of the football team
Coach Carter	True story of controversial high school basketball coach Ken Carter

Find Everyday Heroes

When you were growing up, did you have a hero? My nephew loves the Hulk, at least right now. Part of what he likes is that the Hulk is "big and strong and green and he has purple pants; he gets the bad guys." Children need heroes they can admire; that's a normal part of growing up. In fact, in a world full of negativity, we all need heroes. One of the lessons we learned from September 11, 2001, was that heroes can be normal people who do what they can to help others, such as firefighters and police officers. You can motivate yourself by reminding yourself of the everyday teacher-heroes in your life.

My list starts with my father, a coach and a retired university professor who has always taught—his children, his students, and everyone around him. His lessons to me are still powerful: It's important to care about every single student you teach; it's more important to do the right thing than it is to be right all the time. I learned one of his most powerful lessons at a basketball game when I was in high school, and he was the referee. I went with him to a game; and while sitting in the stands, I listened to fans yell at him throughout the entire game. Nothing he did was right, and they called him stupid and some other things that I won't repeat. I was in tears. After the game, he just smiled and said that he never even heard what they said; he just did his job and ignored the rest.

That powerful lesson has stayed with me today in two ways. First, even though I am a rabid college basketball fan, I never yell at the referees. Second, when things get tough, I know I need to do my job and ignore the rest; particularly the unwarranted criticism that can come from those who think they know more about a situation than they do. If I had a dollar for every time someone told me that I couldn't write a book, it was too hard, or someone might not like it, I'd be rich! But none of that was important. I kept my focus, I did my job writing, and I was successful; all the while applying the long-taught lesson from my dad.

The teachers I work with regularly are heroes who daily do whatever they can to make a difference with their students. Although there are too many to list, I want to tell you about Marie. She came into my class one night and was quieter than usual. That day she had found a *flip book*, which is a notebook in which students had written death threats to the teacher. She was convinced that the student in whose desk it was found was innocent, but she couldn't imagine who would have done this. The notebook was filled with comments no teacher should ever have to read. I sent her home and talked with her every day that week. What struck me the most was that, throughout all of her fear and frustration, she still was optimistic about that student's potential. She also never really considered not teaching her students. What does it take to face down fear? It takes the heart of a hero, and that's what teachers have. Who is on your list?

Think About It...

Who are the everyday heroes in your life?

Surround Yourself With Motivating Thoughts

Another important thing I do is create an environment filled with motivating thoughts and pictures. I collect quotes by famous and not-so-famous people on a variety of motivational topics such as persistence, success, and focus. I write some of them in my journal, I put some of then up on my bulletin board or my computer screen, my file cabinet, desk, or anywhere else where I will see them regularly. I've even changed my screen saver at work so the scrolling text is my quote of the moment; the one that I'm most enamored with each week. I set my background on my computer desktop to be a picture of something that reminds me of what is most important to me. Right now, it's a collage of pictures of my niece and nephew. No matter how crazy it gets at work, I can look at their smiling faces and everything seems a little better. I receive a daily motivation quote by e-mail, which guarantees that no matter how much junk e-mail I get, no matter how many problems people want me to solve, I always get at least one encouraging e-mail per day. I also set my home page to a Web page with motivational thoughts. Again, this forces me at least once, when I log on to the Internet, to see something positive and uplifting.

Keep a Success Journal

Journaling is a practice that I still struggle to incorporate in my life, but I have found it to be one of the most critical parts of self-reflection. If the idea of writing pages and pages of daily events doesn't thrill you, don't worry. That's not what I'm talking about. I suggest keeping a list of successes that happen each day, a log of good things that happen. Challenge yourself to write down something positive every day. Even if it's nothing more than that you survived today, write it down. Maybe Billy smiled at you for the first time, or Hakim showed up, or Serena brought her homework. Keep the list and keep writing it down. The discipline itself will motivate you, and keeping it in a journal allows you to revisit it on the stressful days. The success journal is also a great place to keep your list of books and movies and to log and describe your everyday heroes. Keep it with your Memory File, and you have instant inspiration anytime you need it. Just don't forget to look at them frequently.

Make the Choice—Every Day

Ultimately, motivating yourself is about making a choice every single day that you are going to do your best, and you are going to stay positive—no matter what. It may be just remembering that you do make a difference. Or it may be continuing to do your job, even when the crowd is yelling at you. It is going in every day to teach, even when you don't see that you are making a difference. It's believing the best, even when the students don't act their best. One thing that great teachers have in common is that they keep themselves motivated and they do whatever it takes to make that happen.

The *X-factor* is giving yourself a daily dose of motivation. Make the commitment now to starting every day off RIGHT!

R	Remind yourself of why you do this.
I	Invest energy in positive activities.
G	Grin—it's contagious.
H	Hang out with positive people.
T	Take time to reflect and renew.

Summary

- Motivate yourself! If you are not motivated, your students won't be either.
- Inspire yourself daily!
- Keep inspirational e-mails, pictures, or letters in a special place and pull them out when you need encouragement.
- Read books and watch movies that inspire you to be a better person and teacher.
- Watch movies that remind you of what you don't want to be.
- Find your everyday heroes. You need people you can look up to just like your students do.
- Surround yourself with motivating thoughts. Create positive, encouraging environments in your classroom and home.

- Begin a journal to keep track of your personal victories. Teachers are the most modest people. Counting your successes is important.

- Make the choice every day to do your best and stay positive, no matter what!

If you would like more information...

This site contains motivating quotes: http://www.motivateus.com/.

Great Quotes for Great Educators by Todd Whitaker and Dale Lumpa, Eye On Education.

Rainbows, Head Lice, and Pea-Green Tile by Brod Bagert, Maupin House.

Teachers With Class: True Stories of Great Teachers by Marsha Serling Goldberg and Sonia Feldman, Andrews McMeel Publishing.

Y

You Are the Key

On your worst day, you are someone's best hope.

Sam Myers

Imagine an instance when you were 100% excited about making a difference for kids, the moment you were most enthusiastic about being a teacher. It might be right now, or it may have been a while since you felt that way. Remember the time you totally believed you would change your students' lives? Take a sheet of paper and cut out a heart (yes, red paper would be nice). That was your heart for teaching at that moment. And now, I want you to think about what has happened since then:

- You read the fiftieth news story about how overpaid teachers are. (Go ahead, rip off a piece of the heart and throw it on the floor. That's how it felt, right?)

- You poured your heart and soul into the student everyone said was a lost cause, only to have the parents come to school and berate you for not doing enough. (Rip off another piece.)

- A teacher told you it was nice that you had all these ideas about helping kids but that it's really all about the test scores. (*Rrrrrrrrip!*)

- Extra duties and paperwork seem to fill all the extra times. (*Rip!*)

- You were told that you can't take the kids on a field trip because it wasn't "instructional." (*Rip.*)
- Some days and weeks you are just so tired that you can't move because you are working harder than you ever knew you could, and you just aren't seeing that you are making a difference. (*Rip.*)
- Fill in the blank with your own experience. (*Rip.*)

Wow! How much of your heart is left? You may feel like you need a heart transplant. I had periods of time when I felt disheartened, particularly at the end of my first year of teaching. I also had days when I started the morning full of energy and passion and excitement, but by 10 a.m. the problems dragged me down. There were days when it seemed like it didn't really matter if I tried, put forth extra effort, did a really great activity instead of a worksheet, or tried for the hundredth time to reach *that student*. I tried to make a difference, but Roger still got in a fight. I did everything possible, but Brittany still didn't bring her homework. I communicated with parents, but they still said it was my fault that their child wasn't learning.

You probably also have days when you ask, "Is it worth the effort? Am I making a difference?" Let me assure you, you do make a difference. However, one of the most difficult aspects of being a teacher is that we sometimes don't see the results of our efforts. It's like planting an apple tree in your backyard, and discovering you are moving away at the end of the year. Full growth won't be evident until after you are gone. You dug the hole, planted the tree, watered it, added fertilizer and some TLC, but because it takes 3 to 5 years for an apple tree to grow to full height, someone else will enjoy the apples.

Teaching is exactly like that. You invest lots of time, energy, and passion today, but you have to trust that the fruits of your labor will flourish sometime in the future. You do the work and you trust there is a benefit in the future. It's important that every single day, you keep the faith. Your kids watch you; they read your moods; and they notice what you wear, what you say, and even sometimes what you think! And every single day, every single moment, remember, "On your worst day, you are still someone's best hope." You are still their teacher. You—and you alone—are the key to someone learning today.

Also remember that just like your heart is sometimes torn, so are the hearts of your kids. Their hearts are torn by things like mom or dad yelling at them; being late for the bus and having to find a way to get to school; another kid laughing at them because their shirt isn't the *cool one*, not getting breakfast; not getting enough sleep because dad and his girlfriend had a fight; having to take care of a two-year old sibling because mom is working two jobs;

not getting homework done because there wasn't time to go to the library after work…. The list is endless. For those students you may be the only person who says they are good at something. You may be the only person who asks, "What do you think"? You may be the only one who asks, "How can I help?" You may be the only person who says, "Great job!" You may be the only one who says, "No, that wasn't right, but I know you can do it if you try again."

Cameron, one of my graduate students, teaches science in a middle school. He tells the story of Melvin, a student with poor grades who often got into trouble. When he was reprimanded by his teachers, Melvin would roll his eyes and smack his lips.

As Cameron explains, "One day I saw Melvin in the restroom, and I noticed that he took time to wash his hands thoroughly. In class, we were discussing Fungi and Bacteria. During this unit, I mentioned the importance of washing your hands properly. This was during the time of year when many students begin to get sick. I did not say anything to him about how good of a job he did washing his hands that day; in fact, I did not even let him know that I recognized it. The next day in class I used him as an example. A smile came on his face and from that day forward his grades began to steadily increase, his undesirable behavior decreased, and he also began to talk to me more than he did in the past."

Do you still think you don't make a difference to your students? Cameron's story isn't that unusual—it happens to teachers every single hour in classrooms all across the world.

You are the thermometer for your classroom; your students' temperatures rise or fall based on what they see happening with you. Find the energy to make those extra efforts with your students. Now before I go on, you might be thinking that I don't understand; you don't have that much energy anymore. I'm telling you to fake it until you feel it. Your energy, excitement, and enthusiasm will drive the levels of your students. Make the decision to take one action every day to positively impact your students:

- Smile today, even if you don't feel like it.
- Find your quietest students and ask about their days.
- Say something positive about your worst student.
- Refuse to allow "I can't" to be uttered by anyone, including yourself.

Then, when that's working, decide to do two things, then three, and then you're on such a roll that you can't stop yourself (and really, you are the only one who can). You feel like you are told by everyone else what to teach, when to teach, and how to teach? I understand. But figure out how to make a difference within that environment anyway. Even if you have to follow a script, you choose your level of enthusiasm, your voice tone, and your facial expressions. If you can't take a field trip because of regulations, bring one into the classroom through technology, video, or guest speaker. Do you feel like there's so much emphasis on testing that you don't get to do anything fun? That simply isn't true. Fun is a state of mind.

Are you beginning to get the idea? Deciding whether or not you want to be the key isn't a choice—you *are* the key for your students. Your choice is whether you want to be a bright, shiny key that opens new doors of learning for your students or a rusty key that is worn down by all the problems. And it is your choice every single day, every single moment. In a flash of a second, you choose to smile or frown, breathe deeply or yell, hand out a worksheet and make everyone sit and write silently or allow students to work together. I developed a simple acronym to focus on the key elements teachers can bring to the classroom:

Choice

C	Commitment
H	High energy
O	Optimism
I	Intensity
C	Confidence
E	Enthusiasm

Are you willing to make the commitment to be the key for each student you teach? Will you bring a high energy to your class each day and raise your level of energy when your students' levels are lower? Will you always be optimistic, believing that you are making a difference and that every student you teach can learn and improve every day? Will you bring intensity and focus to your work? And finally, will you be enthusiastic and positive about your students, yourself, and learning? Actually, every single day is a great day! Do you believe that? And do you share that belief with everyone around you?

It is easy to focus on test scores as the only measure of your success. And it's not hard to fall into the belief that you aren't valued. But I would challenge you to decide what you believe. Do you believe you make a difference? If so, make the *choice* to impact your students every day. As a reminder, post the story below where you can see it. It was sent to me in an e-mail, and it's a great summary for this chapter. It's an excerpt of poem adaptation by Taylor Mali (http://www.taylormali.com), and I share it with you with his permission.

What Does a Teacher Make?

The dinner guests were sitting around the table discussing life. One man, a CEO, decided to explain the problem with education. He argued, "What's a kid going to learn from someone who decided his best option in life was to become a teacher?" He reminded the other dinner guests what they say about teachers: "Those who can do. Those who can't teach." To corroborate, he said to another guest: "You're a teacher, Susan. Be honest. What do you make?"

Susan, who had a reputation of honesty and frankness, replied, "You want to know what I make? I make kids work harder than they ever thought they could. I can make a C+ feel like a Congressional Medal of Honor....You want to know what I make? I make kids wonder. I make them question. I make them criticize. I make them apologize and mean it. I make them write. I make them read, read, read....I make them show all their work in math and hide it all on their final drafts in English. I make them understand that if you have the brains, then follow your heart... and if someone ever tries to judge you by what you make, you pay them no attention. You want to know what I make? I make a difference. What about you?"

Summary

- On your worst day, you are still someone's best hope.
- Every little thing you say and do each and every day *does* make a difference to the students in your life.
- You are the thermometer in your classroom. Find the energy to make extra efforts with you students.
- Sometimes, on a bad day, you have to fake the energy and enthusiasm until you truly feel it.
- You can make the commitment to establish an enthusiastic and optimistic environment for your students. Provide an intense, high-energy atmosphere that builds self-confidence. It's your *choice*!

If you would like more information…

A site full of inspiration for teachers: http://www.inspiring teachers.com/inspirations/.

A Cup of Comfort for Teachers edited by Colleen Sell, Adams Media.

Stories of Courage to Teach: Honoring the Teacher's Heart by Sam M. Intrator, Jossey-Bass.

Teacher: The One Who Made the Difference by Mark Edmundson, Vintage Books.

Teaching with Love, Laughter, and Lemonade by Paul S. Bodner, Dad's Lemonade Stand.

Why We Teach edited by Sonia Nieto, Teachers College Press.

Z

On Beyond Zebra

There are things beyond Z that most people don't know.

Dr. Seuss

Think About It...

Where do you go from here?

One of my favorite books is *On Beyond Zebra* by Dr. Seuss. It is the story of Conrad Cornelius o'Donald o'Dell, a young boy who is learning to spell. As he writes and describes each letter of the alphabet, he finishes with Z for Zebra and says to the author of the story: "So now I know everything anyone knows from beginning to end. From the start to the close. Because Z is as far as the alphabet goes."

You may feel like Conrad; you are at the end of this book, and you have a wealth of strategies for building a motivating environment for your students. You now know how to Begin With the End in Mind and about Forming Partnerships. You understand the importance of not Jumping to Conclusions and encouraging your students to Never Give Anyone Permission to Take Away Your Chance for Success. And now you are at Z, which would be the end of the alphabet and this book.

However, you have not arrived at the end at all; you are at the beginning of a journey. Along with your students, you are traveling to higher levels of motivation and student involvement than ever before. You see, the main character in *On Beyond Zebra* quickly responds. He tells Conrad that most people stop with Z, "but not me! In the places I go there are things that I see that I never could spell if I stopped with the Z. I'm telling you this 'cause you're one of my friends. *My* alphabet starts where *your* alphabet ends!"

That's what I believe about the strategies in this book. This book is not designed to limit you; each of the strategies I suggested is a signpost pointing the way. You will take your students beyond the ideas I've shared. You will make them your own. As a teacher, you will choose one or more of the ideas, work with it, adjust it, and develop the perfect strategy for your students for a specific situation. That is the artistry of teaching.

And when you do that, e-mail me your story; I want to hear from you and your students. I believe that one of the most important characteristics we share as teachers is that we learn from each other. I've already started collecting stories for the follow-up to this book. As I wrote this book I discovered that I had many more stories to share. Some are from my own teaching experiences; some are from other teachers as I've shared the drafts of the book with them. So, I am already organizing material for my next book.

Did you create a game that is terrific for reviewing vocabulary? Or maybe you and your students created opportunities for students to have voice, choice, and leadership in new and exciting ways? Perhaps you have a story about a special student who achieved with your help despite obstacles. Many of the teachers in this book said, "I don't think what I do is that special. Are you sure anyone would really want to read about it?" I disagree. You don't know until you try. So, send me your stories, or send me the words of your students. I want to know about your journey, and I want to share that with other teachers.

I'd like to leave you with a final note of encouragement. You may be discouraged, or tired, or just wondering if anything that isn't on a test matters anymore. You might be a new teacher feeling overwhelmed and wondering if you have made the right choice as to a profession. Let me reassure you: You are not alone. I have felt that way at times and so have many of the teachers you have met in this book. But your students need you to hope despite the circumstances. They need you to light a path for them.

Use this book to help you, even if you aren't sure anything can help. Decide to create a more motivating environment in your classroom. As Kendra Alston said, "If you believe in something, it will come." Take the first step, and help your students take those first steps. When you do that, you'll discover a world that Dr. Seuss foretold: "There are things beyond Z that most people don't know."

> To share your stories contact Barbara at http://www.barbara blackburnonline.com/.

Summary

- Every end is only a new beginning.
- The information in this book can be used as a stepping stone to success. It is not designed to limit you but to point you toward new beginnings.
- Teaching is an art. You must perfect it each and every day with the individual challenges your students bring to the class.
- Your colleagues are your best source for ideas, advice, and inspiration. Learn from one another. Share your unique story with others.

Bibliography

Allen, D. (2001). *Getting things done: The art of stress-free productivity.* New York: Penguin Group.

Allen, J. (2004). *Tools for teaching content literacy.* United States: Stenhouse.

Anderson, L., & Krathwohl, D. (Eds.). (2001). *A taxonomy for learning, teaching, and assessing: A revision of Bloom's taxonomy of educational objectives.* United States: Addison Wesley Longman.

Armstrong, T. (2000). *Multiple intelligences in the classroom* (2nd ed.). Alexandria, VA: ASCD.

Billmeyer, R., & Barton, M. L. (1998). *Teaching reading in the content areas: If not me, then who?* (2nd ed.). Alexandria, VA: ASCD.

Blackburn, B., McNulty, C., & Peck, S. (n.d.). *Workforce development: Incorporating workforce development activities into the classroom curriculum can create a valuable learning opportunity for middle school students.* Retrieved August 10, 2005, from http://www.acteonline.org/members/techniques/mar03_story4.cfm

Blackburn, B., & Norton, T. (2004, Spring). Content area literacy: One district's efforts to integrate reading and writing across the curriculum. *South Carolina Middle School Association Journal, 13–15.*

Breaux, A. (2005). *The poetry of Annette Breaux.* Larchmont, NY: Eye On Education.

Calkins, L. (1997, April). 3 Ways to help your students become strategic readers. *Instructor, (106)* 7, 40–41.

Clark, R. (2003). *The essential 55: An award-winning educator's rules for discovering the successful students in every child.* New York: Hyperion.

Clark, R. (2004). *The excellent 11: Qualities teachers and parents use to motivate, inspire, and educate children.* New York: Hyperion.

Cole, A. (2002). *Better answers: Written performance that looks good and sounds smart.* Portland, ME: Stenhouse.

Court TV's Choices and Consequences. (n.d.). *Safe passage: Voices from the middle school.* Retrieved June 18, 2005, from http://www.courttv.com/safe passage/start3.html?sect=2

Covey, S. R. (1989). *The seven habits of highly effective people.* New York: Simon and Schuster.

Creating S.M.A.R.T Goals. (n.d.). Retrieved August 14, 2005, from www.topachievement.com/smart.html

Cunningham, P., & Allington, R. (1999). *Classrooms that work: They can all read and write* (2nd ed.). United States of America: Addison-Wesley Educational.

Davis, B. (1999). *Motivating students.* Retrieved April 8, 2005, from http://honolulu.hawaii.edu/intranet/committees/FacDevCom/guidebk/teachtip/quizzes. htm

Deckers, L. (2005). *Motivation: biological, psychological, and environmental* (2nd ed.). United States of America: Pearson Education.

Dinkmeyer, D., & Losoncy, L. (1980). *The encouragement book: Becoming a positive person.* Englewood Cliffs, NJ: Prentice-Hall.

Donovan, M. S., Bransford, J., & Pellegrino, J. (Eds.) (n.d.) *How people learn: Bridging research and practice.* Retrieved July 3, 2005, from http://www.books.nap.edu/html/howpeople2/ch2.html

Eight Ways of knowing...Exploring multiple intelligences. Retrieved June 8, 2005,from http://www.multi-intell.com/MI_chart.html

Eisenberger, R., & Cameron, J. (1996, November). Detrimental effects of reward: Reality or myth? *American Psychologist, 51,* 1153–1166.

Fielding, L., & Roller, C. (1992, May). Making difficult books accessible and easy books acceptable. *The Reading Teacher, (45)* 9, 678–685.

Frayer, D., Frederick, W., & Klausmeier, H. (1969). *A schema for testing the level of cognitive mastery.* (Working paper #16). Madison, WI: Wisconsin Research and Development Center.

Fulghum, R. (1988). *All I really need to know I learned in kindergarten.* United States: Ballantine Books.

Gaddy, B., Dean, C., & Kendall, J. (n.d.) *Noteworthy Perspectives: Keeping the focus on learning.* (Available from the Mid-continent Research for Education and Learning, 2550 S. Parker Road, Suite 500, Aurora, CO, 80014–1678).

Ginsberg, M., & Wlodkowski, R. (2000). *Creating highly motivating classrooms for all students: A schoolwide approach to powerful teaching with diverse learners.* San Francisco, CA: Jossey-Bass.

Harmin, M. (1994). *Inspiring active learning: A handbook for teachers.* Alexandria, VA: ASCD.

Harvey, S., & Goudvis, A. (2000). *Strategies that work: Teaching comprehension to enhance understanding.* York, ME: Stenhouse.

Hawley, R., & Hawley, I. (1979). *Building motivation in the classroom: A structured approach to building student achievement.* Amherst, MA: Education Research Associates.

Headquarters for Research on Mathematical and Science Study. Retrieved July 16, 2005, from http://www.timss.org

Juster, N. (1989). *The Phantom Tollbooth.* New York: Random House.

Kendall, J., & Khuon, O. (2005). *Making sense: Small-group comprehension lessons for English Language Learners.* Portland, ME: Stenhouse.

Kirschenbaum, H., Simon, S., & Napier, R. (1971). *Wad-ja-get? The grading game in American Education.* New York: Hart.

Kozloff, M. (2002). *Three requirements of effective instruction: Providing sufficient scaffolding, helping students organize and activate knowledge, and sustaining high engaged time.* Wilmington, NC: University of North Carolina at Wilmington, Watson School of Education.

Larkin, M. (2001). Providing support for student independence through scaffolded instruction. *Teaching Exceptional Children, 34,* 30–34.

Lesesne, T. (2003). *Making the match: The right book for the right reader at the right time, grades 4–12.* Portland, ME: Stenhouse.

Literacy across the curriculum: Setting and implementing goals for grades six through 12. Atlanta, GA: SREB.

Mali, T. (n.d.) *Taylor Mali.* Retrieved August 1, 2005, from http://www.taylormali.com/

McCombs, B. (n.d.) *Understanding the keys to motivation to learn.* Retrieved July 3, 2005, from http://www.mcrel.org/fellows/noteworthypages/noteworthy/barbaram.asp

McDonald, J. (1993, October). *Dilemmas of planning backward: Rescuing a good idea.* Retrieved July 8, 2005, from http://www.essentialschools.org/cs/cespr/view/ces_res123

McLeod, J., Fisher, J, & Hoover, G. (2003). *The key elements of classroom motivation: Managing time and space, student behavior, and instructional strategies.* Alexandria, VA: ASCD.

Metametrics. (n.d.). *The 3 R's: Using the Lexile Framework.* Durham, NC: Metametrics.

Mid-continental Research for Education and Learning. (2000, November). *Including special needs students in standards-based reform: A report on McREL's diversity roundtable III.* Aurora, CO: Author.

Pintrich, P., & Schunk, D. (2002). *Motivation in education: Theory, research, and applications* (2nd ed.). Upper Saddle River, NJ: Pearson Education.

Raphael, T. (1986). Teaching question-and-answer relationships, revisited. *Reading Teacher, 39*(6), 516–522.

Reeves, D. B. (n.d.) *The 90/90/90 Schools: A Case Study.* Retrieved June 5, 2005, from http://www.makingstandardswork.com/Downloads/AinA%20Ch19.pdf

Richardson, V. (Ed.). (2001). *Handbook of research on teaching* (4th ed.). Washington, D.C.: American Educational Research Association.

Sagor, R., & Cox, J. (2004). *At-risk students: Reaching and teaching them* (2nd ed.). Larchmont, NY: Eye On Education.

Scaffolding Learning. (n.d.) Retrieved July 3, 2005, from http://www.myread.org/scaffolding.htm

Schlechty, P. (2002). *Working on the work: An action plan for teachers, principals, and superintendents.* San Francisco, CA: Jossey-Bass.

Schomoker, M. (2001). *The results fieldbook: Practical strategies from dramatically improved schools.* Alexandria, VA: ASCD.

Siebold, S. (2005). *101 Secrets of the World Class.* Retrieved August 6, 2005, from http://www.londonhousepress.com

Stipek, D. (2002). *Motivation to learn: Integrating theory and practice* (4th ed.). Boston: Allyn & Bacon.

Strong, R., Silver, H., & Perini, M. (2001). *Teaching what matters most: Standards and strategies for raising student achievement.* Alexandria, VA: ASCD.

Stronge, J. (2002). *Qualities of effective teachers.* Alexandria, VA: ASCD.

Svinicki, M. (2004). *Learning and motivation in the postsecondary classroom.* Wiliston, VT: Anker.

Tomlinson, C. A. (1999). *The differentiated classroom: Responding to the needs of all learners.* Alexandria, VA: ASCD.

Vacca, R., & Vacca, J. (2005). *Content area reading: Literacy and learning across the curriculum.* United States of America: Pearson Education.

Wasserstein, P. (1995, September). What middle schoolers say about their schoolwork. *Educational Leadership, 53,* 41–43.

Weiss, I., & Pasley, J. (2004, February). What is high-quality instruction? *Educational Leadership, (61)* 5,24–28.

Wynn, M., & Blassie, D. (1995). *Building dreams: Elementary school edition.* Marietta, GA: Rising Sun.

Wynn, M. (2001). *Increasing student achievement: Schools of excellence.* Marietta, GA: Rising Sun.